FROM THE Bush TO Brookvale

THE CLIFF LYONS STORY

FROM THE Bush TO Brookvale

THE CLIFF LYONS STORY

ALAN WHITICKER

Published by
Gary Allen Pty Ltd
ACN 002 793 160
9 Cooper Street
Smithfield, NSW 2164
Ph: (02) 9725 2933
Fax: (02) 9609 6106

ISBN 1 875 169 80 6

The National Library of Australia
Cataloguing-in-Publication entry

Whiticker, Alan
From the Bush to Brookvale (the Cliff Lyons Story)

Bibliography
ISBN 1 875 169 80 6

1. Lyons, Cliff   2. Rugby League football players - Australia -
Biography.   3. Rugby League football players - New South
Wales - Biography.   I. Title.

796.3338092

Cover and page design by Paul Martinsen, ɑgraphics

Printed and Bound by Australian Print Group,
Maryborough, Victoria

Dedication

For Karen (CL)
For Karen (AW)

Acknowledgements

There are many people whom we would like to thank for their help in the writing and publishing of this book: Gary Allen, Berith Ostrom, Paul Martinsen, Cliff and Karen Lyons, Melva Kennedy, Colin Lyons, Kevin and Connie Luff, Ken Arthurson, Bob Fulton, Peter Sharp, Steve Stickney, John Morecombe, John Madigan, Pat Sullivan, Clarke Scott, David Liddiard and Ian Collis. Lastly, to my family, thank you for your continued support and good humour during the last six months in order to make yet another deadline.

Photo Credits

About the Author

Alan Whiticker has emerged as one of the most prolific writers of Rugby League history. Since 1988, he has written or co-written seven books on the code, two of which have gone on to a third edition. These are:

The History of the Balmain 'Tigers' (1988), *The History of the North Sydney 'Bears'* (with Greg Anderson, 1988), *The Terry Lamb Story* (1992), *Grand Finals of the NSWRL* (1992, 1994 and 1997), *The Encyclopedia of Rugby League Players* (with Glen Hudson, 1993, 1995 and 1999), *Rugby League Test Matches in Australia* (with Ian Collis, 1994) and *From the Bush to Brookvale – The Cliff Lyons Story* (2000).

Born in Penrith NSW in 1958, Alan attended school at St Dominic's College Kingswood and graduated from Nepean C.A.E (now the University of Western Sydney) in 1979 with a Diploma in Teaching. Since achieving his Bachelor of Education in 1986, Alan has pursued the dual careers of teaching and freelance writing. In 1997, he graduated from the Australian Catholic University with a Masters in Education and is currently the Deputy Principal of a northwestern Sydney Catholic Primary School.

Alan lives in Penrith with his wife Karen and children, Timothy and Melanie.

Contents

Introduction

In the foyer of the Manly-Warringah Rugby League Club there is a framed, signed picture of the top ten players in the 53-year history of the Sea Eagles' club. Terry Randall, Cliff Lyons, Max Krilich, Des Hasler, Fred Jones, Bob Fulton, Graeme Eadie, Alan Thompson, Paul Vautin and Bob Batty – each having played in over 200 first grade games, are pictured together as the record makers of the Manly-Warringah Club. Leading the way, with 309 first grade games to his credit, is Cliff Lyons – a player whose career will shine like a beacon now that the Manly club has entered into a joint venture with North Sydney and been reborn as the Northern Eagles.

I first met Cliff Lyons at Gundagai Racetrack in October 1989. My father's 'country cousins' had spent years researching our family tree and a huge reunion had been organised for the long-weekend. The incorrect spelling of my family's surname *Whiticker*, a mistake attributed to the fact that the first descendants of transported Irish convict George Whitaker (c.1830) could neither read nor write, made it easy to track down the generations that had sprung from the marriage of George's son Richard *Whiticker* and Mary Ann Clark.

The many respective family branches were represented at the reunion with one such branch - the Neiberding's from Adelong, present on that Sunday get-together at Gundagai. Cliff had married a distant cousin of mine, Karen Luff, whom I had never met until the writing of this book.

Cliff was back in Gundagai, having just been part of the disappointing 1989 season in which Manly failed to make the semi-finals, with his wife, her family and their infant daughter and was obviously enjoying a much-needed break from the game. While kicking a football with his in-laws, my wife Karen, a long-time Manly fan, could not resist the temptation to introduce herself and talk to him as if she had known him for years. She gave Cliff a copy of a modest book I had written on the history of the North Sydney Bears, a gift that he accepted with grace and charm.

'Hey, I can show this to my brother-in-law,' he said. 'This proves I scored a try at Norths.'

I was immediately struck by Cliff's good humour and easy-going nature, marvelling at how willing he was to accommodate perfect strangers who wished to talk to him about his career. That is the nature of being in the public eye, I thought – people think that they know you. Having interviewed many players, past and present, in the course of writing seven books on the game during the past ten years, there is a truism in which I firmly believe that states, 'Success magnifies the person you really are.' Cliff, I had always thought, must have been a fairly decent sort of bloke to begin with.

Fast-forward to August 1999 – and the culmination of a tremendous career. As competitive as the National Rugby League is, few players come along in a generation as tough and naturally gifted as Cliff Lyons. Bush bred but city-raised, Lyons matured late in his career to forge his reputation as one of the most durable and skillful players in the modern era.

If careers were built on statistics alone, then Cliff's list of achievements would be sufficient:

- 332 premiership games for Norths and Manly – at the time of writing, second only in total to legendary pivot Terry Lamb (349 matches);
- a club record 309 first grade games with Manly-Warringah – only the second player (behind Andrew Ettingshausen at Cronulla) to surpass the 300 mark with the one club and the only Manly clubman to do so;
- over 50 games for Leeds and the Sheffield Eagles in three seasons of English Club football;
- five appearances for City Seconds, City Firsts and City Origin
- six State of Origin matches for NSW;
- six Tests for Australia – two each against Great Britain, France and Papua-New Guinea, with the undoubted highlight winning the Ashes with the 1990 Kangaroos;
- winner of two premiership titles with the Sea Eagles (1987 & 1996) as well as two runners-up medallions (1995 & 1997);
- two Gold 'Dally M' Awards (1990 & 1994) as well as a First Runners-Up Trophy (1995);
- The Clive Churchill Medal winner (1987); and
- and Aboriginal Sportsman of the Year (1999) – tied with AFL's Nicky Winmar.

Cap his career with the dual honour of captaining the inaugural Aboriginal 'Dream Team' in the World Sevens (1996) and the Australian Aborigines in an unofficial 'Test' against Papua-New Guinea (1999) - and you have the sort of career that most players can only dream about.

But cold, bare statistics tell only part of the Cliff Lyons story.

The second son of six Aboriginal children, Cliff came from the Aboriginal mission of Brungle in southwest NSW to Sydney's outer western suburbs via the backstreets of Newtown and Redfern. However, to simply write that Cliff's family came from abject poverty is to strip his childhood of its soul and meaning. Cliff came from a loving, supportive family who battled incredible hardship and discrimination to establish their independence and self-sufficiency.

'Cliff is obviously proud of his heritage and has never made any effort to be anyone other than who he is,' says Ken Arthurson, the former Executive Chairman of the Australian Rugby League and President of the Manly-Warringah League Club. At Cliff's Testimonial Dinner in 1995, Arthurson wrote:

'Ever since the game of rugby league has been played, young men have been coming down from country towns, jumping the rattler to try their luck in Sydney. Few have done it with more style or sustained success than Cliff Lyons. His first trek – as a teenager linking with the Cronulla Sharks – was in 1981 and pre-dated the Winfield Cup. Cliff then went back and played three seasons in the 'bush' (with the Gundagai Tigers) before his fair dinkum arrival in Sydney, with Norths, in 1985. Anyone in any street in Manly can tell you he first linked with the Sea Eagles in 1986. That Manly just happened to win the premiership the next year was no coincidence – and it was Cliff who took the Clive Churchill Medal in the grand final against Canberra. Ever since he first pulled on the jumper that year, Cliff has been monumentally influential in both *Manly style* and *Manly success.*'

Who then is the *real* Cliff Lyons? Known as '*Napper*' to his team-mates, a nickname given to him by champion coach Bob Fulton, Cliff's siblings prefer to call him '*Rocky*' while those agnostics among the parochial Brookvale Oval crowd who followed his career over 15 seasons have more than once erected signs that stated "*Cliffy is God.*"

In person, Lyons is as clearly enigmatic as he was a player. In preparation for this book, Cliff proved to be as elusive off the field as when playing for his beloved Manly. Just when I thought that I had captured an insight into the character of the man, he would flash a hint of a smile that so many of his opponents must have glimpsed during his career, sidestep an issue and in an instant he would be gone. At times, I was left clutching at his shadow.

The reality anchoring Cliff Lyons' particular story is that he came from an Aboriginal mission in country NSW to represent Australia in the international arena of his chosen sport. Not just any arena, but the highest honour in rugby league – an Ashes contest against Great Britain. In most other countries, this in itself a would be something on which to build a legend, but in Australia where we tend to take these things for granted because we have so many sporting champions, Lyons' achievement went largely unheralded. Cliff's career reflects equally on the nature of the great game of rugby league - a sport which can promote natural ability to the highest levels, and on the character of a man rooted to the ground by his humble beginnings and self-effacing humility.

That is not to say that Cliff does not have his share of ego or natural aggression. Quietly spoken and stony-faced off the field, Lyons nevertheless exudes a personal confidence and charisma. But then all the game's great halves had a healthy regard for their own ability – Tommy Raudonikis, 'Turvey' Mortimer, Wally Lewis, 'Alfie' Langer; and like Terry Lamb or Garry Freeman, stood toe to toe with an opposing forward and taken a smack in the mouth rather than take a backward step on the football field. Lyons though, was that sporting rarity in that he stealthily backed his self-confidence with a raw, almost uncoachable ability and an undeniable will-to-win.

More than that, he enjoyed what he did immensely.

'Cliff is a man for whom I've always had the highest regard,' says Ken Arthurson. 'Life hasn't been easy for him and he's had to do it the tough way. He's come up through the hard school and proven himself to be an outstanding athlete and an outstanding sportsman.

The great thing about the game of rugby league is that the rewards are there if you have the talent and are willing to put the effort into it,' says Arthurson. 'The thing that I've most admired about Cliff is that great will to win - the desire to succeed. If there is any one attribute that I admire in a sportsman, it is the will to win and a determination to do one's best. It just wasn't in Cliff's makeup during his career to go out onto a football field and *not* give his best. He was a very tenacious player who *loved* to win.'

Cliff's sporting career is a blueprint for any bush kid who wants to back his talent with hard work. Former Australian Test player Greg Hawick, the man attributed with bringing Lyons back to Sydney in 1985 says, 'It was no surprise to see Cliff go on and play for Australia. He's an outstanding thinker who was a jump ahead of the rest of the players on the field. His ability to pass and back up without being tackled was just incredible.'

Cliff's family background has a lot to do with his attitude towards his success in rugby league. He always had the talent to be a sportsman, but then so did the rest of his family. 'Clifford was incredibly lucky,' says his mother Melva Kennedy, who raised six children after the break up of her marriage to Cliff's father, Patrick. With Cliff, who is clearly uncomfortable talking about his achievements, there is always an economy of words. As his younger brother Colin told me, 'If you speak to Cliff on the phone, you have to do all the talking. Sometimes you even have to ask him if he's still there.'

Colin remembers, 'It was hard for all of us to get chosen in 'rep' teams, even when I was playing football because we had no one there with us – we had to do it by ourselves on our own ability. Other players trying out for 'reps' would have their fathers and uncles and family and coaches influencing the people picking the teams. Cliff never had any of that. He was just this shy kid with a lot of talent trying to get ahead without promoting or big-noting himself.'

It was Gundagai which gave him a fresh start in rugby league and from where he launched his Sydney career in 1985. After marrying local girl Karen Luff in 1987, Gundagai is now a second home to Cliff and his family. Today, it would be fair to say that Cliff is as synonymous with Gundagai as the dog on the tuckerbox. 'Cliff had to sacrifice a lot to get where he is,' says Colin. 'He sacrificed a lot to go to Sydney and to play with Norths – first he had to change his whole lifestyle into the "professional footballer" mode and that meant that he to break a lot of ties with the bush, the Aboriginal community and with his own family.'

After a successful introduction to Sydney football with Norths in 1985, Cliff signed with Manly. Far too often, Manly has been conveniently labelled 'silvertails' by rival fans but one could never accuse Cliff, rugby league's 'common man,' of ever being that. It is interesting to note that the Sea Eagles had no fewer than five Aboriginal players in its premiership-winning team in 1987 - players as diverse in their talents as their place of origin. Cliff Lyons, Ron Gibbs, Dale Shearer, Mal Cochrane and Paul Shaw – from the Riverina in southwest NSW to Sarina in far North Queensland, Manly followed the well-worn rugby league track of promoting talent from the bush and providing an atmosphere where players could excel at what they did best.

Modestly he says, 'I was doing pretty much the same things at Manly that I had been doing in Gundagai but my timing improved and I had more talented players running off me. I was extremely lucky that I had players like Michael O'Connor, Steve Menzies and Terry Hill who could read the game.' There's that word again – *lucky*. But luck can carry you only so far; the will to succeed comes from deep within.

Cliff regards his Manly and Australian Test coach Bob Fulton as having the greatest influence on his professional career. 'As a coach, Bob would pull you aside and tell you certain things about your game, but once you took the field the rest had to come from you – from inside. There are obviously things that happen out on the football field that you can't train for and "Bozo" always encouraged me to take the opportunities when they presented them. But what he told you really stuck with you during a match.'

The same can be said about life, and more than once Bob Fulton has had a quiet word with Cliff about addressing life issues. 'I consider Cliff a close friend,' says Fulton. 'I have an enormous amount of time and respect for the guy. He has the ability and charisma to be a role model for kids, especially in the Aboriginal community, and he has never ventured that far from 'the bush'. I have taken Cliffy away hunting on our family farm on several occasions and he's in his element up there. He just loves the place.'

That personal side of Cliff Lyons, the family man, has mostly been hidden from the public.

Cliff's mother, his brother Colin and Bob Fulton have each acknowledged the role Karen Lyons has played in supporting his career. 'Karen has been the biggest single influence in Cliff's life,' says Colin. 'She's been a big influence on the financial side of things too. Cliff would play for nothing if it were up to him, he just loves the game so much.'

'Karen is an extraordinary woman,' says Melva Kennedy. 'She has had to share Cliff with the public and have their married life disrupted to accommodate his profession as a footballer.' One can't help but appreciate Karen's frustration in dealing with a sometimes-uncompromising media and a fickle public that often tears down its sporting heroes as quickly as they're placed on pedestals.

Shane Lyons, Cliff's eldest son and a soccer professional with the Northern Spirit, has always been an important part of Cliff and Karen's life. Brookvale locals have also grown accustomed to the sight of Cliff and his three shadows – children Courtney, Mathew and Gabrielle, ducking into the local TAB, venturing into the Manly

Football Club or conducting a coaching clinic at Brookvale Ov
during the school holidays.

From the Bush to Brookvale is the story of one man's journey th
is not just measured by distance. 'The Cliff Lyons Story' is mor
about the realisation of a dream – the culmination of natural abilit
and personal growth. It deserves to be told.

Alan Whiticker

CHAPTER ONE

Childhood

T hose of us who have grown up with even a rudimentary knowledge of the poetry of 'Banjo' Patterson, who have read the stories of Henry Lawson or sung traditional colonial ballads taught in schools, could be excused for holding a romantic notion of life in 'the bush'. As with most things, the reality is that life in country Australia is harsh. The uncompromising natural elements, combined with the social constraints of insular town communities, can strip people of their individuality and, in the case of marginal cultural groups, remove their dignity as a people.

It is a cold, hard fact of life that in many parts of rural Australia whole Aboriginal communities have been alienated from society in what can only be viewed as a form of socially enforced apartheid. This is the unpalatable truth ignored by many Australians; an unwelcome mirror into which we have only recently dared look. While it is easy to dismiss this and say that this is no different from urban New York, with its slums and ethnic ghettos, or in England, where cities such as Brixton and Manchester have experienced race violence, this is *our* particular shame as a nation. Aboriginal communities have been, and continue to be, disenfranchised from the same opportunities that mainstream 'white' Australia enjoys - and that is a fact of history that a hundred years of reconciliation, a thousand apologies from the Prime Minister, and millions of dollars in welfare won't erase.

The term 'fringe dwellers' used by author Nene Gare in the title of her 1950s novel best explains the social condition that has prevailed in the country – Aboriginal people existing on the fringe of society without really being accepted as equitable members. These fringe communities, which were serviced by well-meaning but at times misguided religious and welfare groups, have in many cases become breeding grounds for poverty, ill-health and injustice. As with any marginalised group who cannot see a way out of their situation, poverty in turn leads to crime, alcoholism, domestic violence and even sexual abuse. When the response from government bodies is predominantly bureaucratic, then further problems such as nepotism, cronyism and financial mismanagement arise.

As recently as January 26, 2000, Australian of the Year Sir Gustav Nossal, Deputy Chairman of the Council for Aboriginal Reconciliation and for thirty years directly involved with the World Health Organisation, declared, 'The situation of Aboriginal people – particularly remote, traditional Aboriginal people who live in smaller communities – is in many ways abysmal. The situation in terms of education possibilities, health, housing, the infrastructure – such as having running water in the home – and the attitude which some elements of the judicial system take to them can only be called appalling.'

It was into this social context that Patrick Lyons, Cliff's father, started his family at Narrandera. A picture postcard description of the south-western NSW township, situated on the northern banks of the Murrumbidgee River some 570 km from Sydney, is of a Riverina district devoted to crops, wool, fruit, sheep and cattle. The search for work often took Pat Lyons away from Narrandera but never for too long. Clarke Scott, a cousin of the Lyons family who now works as an Aboriginal Community Liaison Officer with the Wentworthville Health Service, remembers Pat and his brother Warwick coming to live with his family at Warragamba on the outskirts of Penrith in the mid 1950s.

'When my father Doug was working on the construction of Warragamba Dam my grandparents came down to live with us,' Clarke says, 'and then Pat and his brother Warwick stayed with us after they got jobs as labourers at the Dam. Pat was a funny, happy-go-lucky bloke who had a real gift for singing and playing the guitar. He taught us lots of songs and my brother Matthew how to play the guitar and we decided to form a group called "The Opals".' Warwick Lyons is the father of former NSW representative winger Graham Lyons while Pat's musical talent was to have a great impact on the boys. Despite barely being teenagers, the Scott brothers performed on tour with acts such as Jimmy Little and Little Pattie and were featured on the TV show *Bandstand* in the 1960s.

When Pat Lyons returned home, he met teenager Melva Kennedy when she was visiting Narrandera with her grandmother. They married and after the birth of their first child, Ricky in 1960, Clifford Patrick Lyons was born on October 19, 1961. Of her second son, Cliff, Melva says, 'I'm the only person who calls him Clifford. Paul Vautin even said on national TV that only his mother is allowed to call him Clifford. He was named after a friend of my husband's but as it later turned out, my great-grandfather's name was Clifford but I only found that out a number of years ago. Clifford was born in Narrandera but he didn't grow up there. When he was four years old, we moved to Brungle on the outskirts of Tumut. We stayed there for about four years and Clifford went to school there.'

The family had grown to five children following the birth of Cliff's younger brother Colin and sisters Narelle and Nita but after Pat and Melva's marriage faltered, Cliff's mother moved the children to Brungle. Somewhat symbolically, Brungle, the Aboriginal community to which Melva Kennedy took her young family in the mid-1960s, is situated 'on the back road' midway between Tumut and Gundagai.

Colin Lyons remembers Brungle fondly, the way most of us would like to recall our childhood. 'To us, Brungle was the best place in the world,' he says without the slightest hint of irony. 'The home we lived in was a tin shack with three walls and a fireplace. It had a dirt floor and our bedroom was one room. We had a three-quarter-size bed and all the kids slept in that. Mum slept in the other room. The only running water there was a tap beside the shack but there was only one or two taps in the whole community. There was a dairy at the back and we used to fill used bottles for two cents. It was tough, but the community was very close-knit and pulled together. We borrowed clothes from neighbours and shared what little we had. I still refer to people from Brungle as relations even if they were relatives of our in-laws.'

The older Lyons children, Ricky, Cliff and Colin, went to school at Brungle. 'Two teachers worked and lived in the community,' says Cliff. 'Kindergarten to Sixth Class was in one room, about fifty kids in all, while the headmaster taught the older kids.' Although the tin sheds have now been replaced by fibro, timber and brick houses, Brungle has again been in the local news recently when the sixty inhabitants complained to Tumut Council about the quality of the drinking water being supplied there.

Brungle also had a football field of sorts and despite its uneven nature and pronounced slope, the locals fielded a rugby league team in Tumut's junior rugby league competition, the Roddy Shield. According to local historian John Madigan, who with brother Bede helped organise the competition in 1946 to accommodate the influx of returned servicemen who wished to resume playing the game, Brungle made a trio of grand final appearances in 1959-61, winning back-to-back premierships in the latter years. In 1965, the year Cliff's family moved there, Brungle was beaten 2-0 in the grand final.

Cliff's mother remembers a young boy who was not scared to try something new. 'In the country, he played a bit of everything – he's even got ribbons for bull-riding!' she says. Cliff though, was not an early starter to the game. 'I didn't play rugby league until I moved to Tregear in Sydney's western suburbs,' remembers Cliff. 'In the bush, I was too busy swimming with the other kids or kicking a ball around with my brothers and cousins – soccer or Aussie Rules usually, but I never played in a rugby league team until I went to Sydney.'

However Melva Kennedy, the single mother of six children following the birth of her son Darren, knew that life in the bush held little promise for her and her children and she decided to take her family to Sydney. 'When we came back to Sydney the family lived in a little house in Newtown before moving to Pitt Street, Redfern,' Melva recalls. 'I always wanted to return to Newtown because I had lived there with my Nan after my mother died. I loved the area and I knew that there was much more opportunity for us. We moved to Newtown with a mobful of kids and of course the landlord didn't want us to stay too long so the lease wasn't renewed after six months. We finally got into a house at Pitt Street but it was old and run down and the roof collapsed on us.'

'That house had holes everywhere,' says Cliff's brother Colin. 'It was a two-storey building but the roof leaked so bad that it even soaked the lounge room on the bottom floor and then the power would blow.'

While living in Redfern, Melva remembers receiving a knock on the door one day and being confronted with an upset son, his face covered in blood, flanked by two strangers. 'There was Clifford, his mouth bleeding and skin all off him and tears running down his face. Two men who didn't speak English very well were trying to explain to me that he had been hit by a car and had landed face down in the street. I thought they meant that they had knocked him down! The police were called and details of the car were taken down. Cliff asked the policeman if he was going to be on TV but he said, "No son, only if you're dead!"'

Colin Lyons also recalls a moment from their childhood that defines their relationship as brothers. 'Something strange happened to us when we were living at Redfern. We were playing with a billycart and I was sitting in it and Cliff was pulling me up the road. As we made our way to the top of the street, in an instant *he* was in the billycart and I was pulling him. We don't know how it happened but almost magically, we had changed places by the time we got to the end. We still talk about it today. It became symbolic of what our adult life was to be like. What made it even stranger was that the building in front of where we were playing was where I was later employed as a drug and alcohol counsellor and youth worker.'

In order to secure public housing, the Lyons family moved to Tregear in 1973 when Cliff was going into Grade 6. 'It's tough for any kid to come into a new school and make friends,' says Colin, 'but we were one of the first Aboriginal families to move into the area and we copped our share of racism. We learned to fight pretty quickly. At school, Cliff was a quiet kid who stuck pretty much to himself.' That was until Cliff discovered rugby league.

'Although there was some connection with rugby league in the country, we weren't really rugby league followers,' says Melva. 'Clifford was the first member of the family to play League and he was a late starter compared to most kids. One day he came home to the family house in Tregear and said that he needed twenty cents. Now, twenty cents was a lot of money in those days and I rarely had it to spare. I asked him what he needed twenty cents for and that's when he said he wanted to play footy. This was the first time that I had heard about it so I went down to the local oval and met the coaches and saw what was going on. Each week you had to pay twenty cents in order to play for the Tregear Foxes. So, I allowed him to play.'

Not surprisingly, there is some conjecture from the Lyons family about who played rugby league first. 'I recall Rick used to play for the 7 stone 2s and he says that he was the first to play footy,' says Colin Lyons. 'We used to go to Redfern Oval to see South Sydney play but we didn't really follow the game. Cliff started off in the Under 12s and after watching him play for a year, I started playing the year after. And the way I remember it,' adds Colin, 'all the kids had to pay twenty cents a game but Cliff was so good the coach used to *give* Cliff twenty cents a game to play.'

Cliff's first coach was a Mr Pickett who made every effort to pick Cliff up at home and get him to the matches. 'That's where football helped all of us at Tregear in that it opened up the social side of things and allowed us to be who we are,' says Colin. He adds, 'Everyone loved to have Cliff on their team.'

Cliff was a natural and learned quickly. 'He found a book on how to play rugby league written by Johnny Raper,' says Melva. 'He took it with him everywhere and read it from cover to cover.' rugby league gave him structure and rules, training and discipline. It gave him an arena to develop his talents and he excelled because he could think quickly on his feet and possessed exceptional ball skills. rugby league became an obsession. 'Soon I had no grass at all on my front lawn,' recalls Melva. 'Every neighborhood kid in the street would come and play rugby league at our house. Clifford would also play against his brothers and sisters – even pulling young Darren out of his cot to take his place in the team.'

Cliff attended school at Tregear Public School with his brothers and sisters, completing the final year of his primary school education. With eldest son Rick already starting high school in the area, Melva Kennedy thought long and hard about the educational opportunities for her other children. Cliff had a natural sporting ability and so she looked to schools that would nurture his talents while providing a stable education. It was then that she heard about Kirinari Youth Centre, an Aboriginal boarding hostel at Sylvania that took in kids from the bush and sent them to local high schools in the Cronulla area.

However, having battled to keep her family together after the break-up of a difficult marriage, sending Cliff away to a boarding hostel originally went against her better judgement. 'I thought it was a great opportunity for Clifford at the time but looking back on it now I would not have let him go because it separated us as a family and, for a time, created a type of division between him and the other kids,' she says. 'The educational opportunity that I thought he would get wasn't there at that time. I wasn't happy with how the place was being run. But it was a good opportunity for him in some ways because he became connected to the Cronulla area and he eventually got to play with Cronulla Under 23s'.

At age 12, Cliff didn't fully understand the decision to send him away from the family home and although he originally hated going to Kirinari, he grabbed any opportunity to play sport – especially Aussie Rules and rugby league. But when he returned home, Cliff noted a change in the relationship between he and his brothers and sisters. 'The other kids asked why he was allowed to go to Kirinari and they weren't,' recalls Melva. 'When he came home, Clifford felt that the other kids didn't want to talk to him. I said to him that I thought that they might have been a little bit jealous of him. "Jealous?" he said. "Mum I don't want to go to Kirinari. I'd rather be home here with them!"'

Brother Colin, who has referred kids to Kirinari in his job as a youth worker in the Bonnyrigg area, says, 'We didn't like it at all because we missed him. He would come home on weekends but if he had sport, we wouldn't see him for weeks on end. Cliff grew away from us.'

Cliff was playing Australian Rules on Saturday and rugby league on Sunday and was training four nights a week. At weekends he would play rugby league with local clubs Caringbah-Cronulla, Sylvania and Gymeah, changing from year to year to play with different groups of friends. Cliff hated boarding school, and so he spent many of his weekends at the home of school friend Glen Sheriden. 'It got to the point where he was training almost every night of the week and he was playing up to three games a week,' says Melva. 'Clifford came home most weekends but it was clear that he didn't want to stay in school. He would rather have been out earning a living.'

'He was remarkable player, even at that stage of his career,' recalls Colin who used to travel down to Cronulla with the rest of the family to watch Cliff play. 'I remember when Cliff tackled someone, they stayed tackled. They didn't want to get up. It was his style of tackling more than any one thing - he would just crunch his opponents. Everybody knows about his ball skills but it was his tackling ability that a lot of people underrate. I saw him week after week deliberately, but not illegally, size up and take out the best players in the opposing side – the bigger, maturer blokes – by tackling them into the ground.'

In his teenage years, Cliff cultivated quite a cult following in the Cronulla juniors. After a clash of heads in a match in which a player remarked that Cliff's head was as hard as a rock, his team-mates started calling him 'Rocky'. The local fans soon caught on as did his family. 'I remember going out to watch him play in the Cronulla competition while he was still at school, says Melva, 'and there was an elderly couple there who came up and introduced themselves to me. They asked me what did I think of his nickname, 'Rocky'? They said that they had named him after boxer Rocky Gattelari!' And so the legend grew. It was not the last time Cliff's head would earn him a nickname and his siblings still often call him 'Rocky'.

In 1981, Cliff was graded by Cronulla in the Shark's Under 23s team as a lock or second row forward. 'I really admired Greg Pierce when I was going to High School in the late 1970s and I modelled my early career on his style of play,' says Cliff. 'Greg had retired as a player and was the first grade coach in 1981 but he still looked incredibly fit.' Signing for $25 a win, Cliff won the club's Best and Fairest Award for Under 23s in his inaugural year and even managed to sit on the first grade bench on several occasions but without making it out onto the field.

'Cliff had an enormous following at Cronulla,' says Colin Lyons. 'He used to sign autographs as 'Kurt Sorensen' - not only because Cliff looked like him but because people thought he was a first grader. Cliff always carried himself like a first grader and had a first grade player's physique.' However there is a tinge of guilt in Colin's recollection of events. 'Our brother Rick was playing for the Miranda Magpies and I was living with Cliff at Cronulla. It was Rick's 21st birthday and I talked Cliff into driving to Narrandera to pick up our grandmother for the party. He missed a training session and the club put him on the bench for Under 23s for the remainder of season.'

Still a teenager, Cliff had been subject to a lot of pressure and change in a relatively short amount of time since leaving school and when his family returned to the Riverina for a holiday at the end of 1981, he chose to follow them. Cliff returned to the bush – a place somewhere between Tumut and Gundagai.

CHAPTER TWO

Gundagai

Gundagai, more than any other country town, has maintained a special place in the history and folklore of this country. Situated on the banks of the Murrumbidgee River 385 km southwest of Sydney, explorers Hume and Hovell and rivermen Sturt and Mitchell opened up the area that was to become a favourite stop-over for travellers on their way to Melbourne. In 1852, after the worst flood disaster in Australian history claimed 80 lives and destroyed over 70 buildings, the town of Gundagai was rebuilt higher on the slopes of Mount Parnassus.

In a district frequented by bushrangers Ben Hall and Captain Moonlight and made famous by Frank Rusconi's sculpture, the Dog on the Tuckerbox at nearby Five Mile Creek, Gundagai has been immortalised in prose and in song from 'Banjo' Patterson and Henry Lawson, to Jack O'Hagan and Steele Rudd. Today Gundagai boasts a modest population of just over 2000 and although the town is by-passed by the Hume Highway, the area remains an important wool and meat-producing centre.

Kevin Luff, Cliff's father-in-law, has been on the land all of his 65 years and in that time, he has seen a lot of changes in Gundagai, saying that, as with everything, 'Some are good and some not so good.' Kevin and wife Connie have seen their property between Gundagai and Adelong grow to some 2000 acres, raising sheep and cattle as well as growing lucerne and wheat. But the Luff's admit that life on the land has more often been a case of feast or famine.

'It's been very tough during the last ten years,' says Kevin Luff. 'The rain that has come in the last twelve months has helped but we could still use a bit more now.' If it's not bad enough battling the natural elements, the downturn in the economy and the rationalisation of the banking industry haven't made life any easier for our primary producers. 'There used to be five banks in town and now there's only one,' he says, 'which doesn't give you a lot of choice. There are a few banking agencies of course but the way they seem to want to go is electronic banking, which of course doesn't suit everybody.'

Gundagai has also played its part in an important piece of Australian Rugby League history. In his excellent book, *The Maher Cup and Tumut*, author John Madigan writes:

From 1921-71, the Maher Cup was the most famous trophy in NSW country rugby league. It had a humble beginning and its demise was forecast years before it gave its last gasp, yet in a life span of over half a century, it became the most coveted cup in the country. It was to rugby league what the Melbourne Cup is to racing. Its fame gained on and off the field was instrumental in laying the foundation of the high standard set and continued in Group 9.

It became a newspaper editor's dream. It had everything. On field action and drama, and off-field controversies as the years unfolded with continuous protests keeping its destiny in the public eye. It was also the medium of big gambling, and huge bets were regularly made on games. The Press, the public and the clubs loved it. During this period, the trophy dubbed.... 'The Old Tin Pot' and

'The Win, Tug and Wrangle Cup'.... was cursed by many and praised by others. It wrecked friendships and was the subject of innumerable writs and lawsuits, and developed into part of the folklore in the South West.'

The Maher Cup was donated by local publican Mr E.J.(Ted) Maher to Tumut District Rugby Union for competition between all rugby union clubs within a radius of 100 miles but this was later extended to 300 miles. The inaugural match for the Maher Challenge Trophy as it was originally known, was played between Tumut and Gundagai on July 4, 1920 under Rugby Union rules. Packing down in the forwards were first cousins George E. Neiberding and Bill Whiticker, the respective grandfathers of Karen Lyons and the author.

In 1921, for no apparent reason and with a minimum of fuss, the competition changed to rugby league rules. For the next fifty years teams from Tumut, Gundagai, Cootamundra, Junee, Harden-Murrumburrah, Wagga, West Wyalong, Cowra, Temora, Canowindra, Barmedman, Grenfell and Young competed for the Cup. In 1981, a decade after the demise of the Cup, Cliff Lyons returned to the Riverina district to find himself and establish a career.

'I used to go camping with my sister at Gundagai,' remembers Melva Kennedy. 'It was a favourite spot of ours. At the end of 1981 Cliff decided to come on holidays with us and later we went down to Tumut. Cliff had friends and cousins in Tumut and he tried to get a run in the Group 9 competition, but Tumut said they had too many players. I still believe that decision had more to do with factors other than his ability.'

'Despite the fact that I had played grade for Cronulla, Tumut didn't want to know me,' remembers Cliff. 'Some of my cousins in Tumut tried to get me a run with them but Tumut said that their books were full for 1982.' Today, he remains slightly bemused by the home-town snub. In a fortunate coincidence, Royce George, a former Bathurst forward who had been a team-mate of Cliff's at

Cronulla, was signed as captain-coach of Gundagai for the coming season. Cliff opted to play with Royce George for the Gundagai Tigers.

Melva Kennedy adds, 'My father Horace Kennedy and his brother used to play for Gundagai in that competition so I was glad that Clifford got to play with the Gundagai Tigers. My uncle was a real fan of Clifford's but the sad thing is that he died before he got a chance to see Clifford play in Sydney. He would have loved that.'

In his first year with the club, Cliff played in a variety of positions - centre, five-eighth and lock, as Gundagai made a welcome return to the semi-finals. Lyons was also selected in a Combined Riverina representative team in the first of three consecutive seasons, although frustratingly, always from the reserves bench. Pat Sullivan, the editor of the local paper *'The Gundagai Independent'* and a Board member of the Tigers' club, was consistently amazed at Cliff's non-selection in representative teams. He also says that there were no ulterior motives or secret agenda other than rank stupidity on the part of selectors.

'I am of the firm belief that you could take any normal man from the street and once you made him a selector, all logical thought and reason would go out the window,' Sullivan told me. 'Cliff was an out and out champion, even at that stage of his career. He was simply an extraordinary talent. Time and time again, Cliff was overlooked for a starting position in the team and placed on the bench. Thankfully John Hobby, the Riverina coach, knew how good a player Cliff was and got him onto the field as soon as possible.'

In 1983, Gundagai ended a twenty-year premiership drought when they defeated Young 40-14 to clinch the Group 9 competition. Played at Fisher Park, Cootamundra, the Tigers led 14-4 at the break before humbling the 'Cherrypickers' in the second half. Gundagai scored at will late in the match with Cliff Lyons finding many gaps in the Young defence. Lock Tony Hawthorne crossed for three tries, building on the great platform laid by Cliff and second-rower Royce George.

Cliff's country form in 1983 brought him to the attention of talent scouts from Sydney. Jim Huxley, *Rugby League Week* Country NSW editor, travelled to West Wyalong where Cliff was playing in a match for Gundagai to present him with a media award and was immensely impressed with what he saw. 'I recommended him to Arthur Beetson at Easts but the Roosters passed on the offer,' Huxley reported after Lyons had made his name in Sydney. But it was only a matter of time before the word got out about Lyons' ability. A Tumut newspaper reported that Lyons would be playing with the Canberra Raiders in 1984. The story apparently originated from a trial Cliff played at Canberra to select the team to play in an Aboriginal knockout competition. At the end of the year, Cliff played a starring role with his brothers Ricky and Colin in Koori United's win in the Koori Knockout competition at Dubbo.

Lyons first came to the attention of former Australian Test pivot Greg Hawick when he was chosen to play for a Wagga Invitation team, ironically against Manly in a pre-season trial in 1984. Brian Dennis, Cliff's Gundagai team-mate, was his partner at inside centre. 'Cliff was in the centres that day,' says Hawick who still lives in Wagga, 'but saved a certain try when he filled in at five-eighth and absolutely hammered his opposing pivot. I thought what a good player this kid was. Cliff was a natural. I had a chat to him after the match and said that he should go to Sydney. I even offered to get him a trial with a club but he was reticent about going up to Sydney by himself.'

Cliff missed the opening four matches of the 1984 Group 9 competition when he was again chosen for Combined Riverina to play in the Caltex Country Cup competition in which Newcastle defeated Riverina in the final. Later that season, and despite losing several players through injury, Gundagai thrashed Wagga Kangaroos in the preliminary final, 26-2. Cliff played in the second row that day and produced a busy and constructive display. Against Young in the grand final, Gundagai suffered a horror run of injuries in the match with Cliff ending up in the front row. Disappointingly, the 'Cherrypickers' turned the tables on their 1983 victors and captured the premiership.

Playing rugby league in Gundagai had given him continuity, maturity, and respect in the local community – and when he became engaged to local dental nurse Karen Luff - emotional stability for the first time in his life. 'When we met there was a lot of opposition to us going out together – obviously it was the difference in cultures,' Karen admits. 'I later encouraged Cliff to go to Sydney because for us at the time, it was all part of the "big adventure". I was ready to leave Gundagai and we thought we'd try living in Sydney for a year.' It wasn't long before the pair would depart, as Banjo Patterson once wrote, 'along the Sydney track'.

In the three years that he lived in Gundagai, Cliff was a frequent visitor to the Luff farm. 'Cliff was a very shy young chap,' remembers Connie Luff, Cliff's mother-in-law. 'He hasn't changed a bit from when he was a twenty-year-old - he's still the lad he was.' Over the past twenty years, Cliff and his family have continually retreated to the farm to visit family and friends, and basically to get away from the pressures of the city. 'There's not much Cliffy can't do on the farm – from shearing sheep to driving a tractor,' says Connie. 'He can turn his hand to almost anything.'

At the end of the 1984, Cliff finished runner-up in polling for the Eric Weissel Medal, the award given to the best and fairest player in the Group 9 competition – a phenomenal effort considering that he missed the early part of the season. The rules were changed after that, giving players a point for any matches they missed because of representative duty. Greg Hawick takes up the story. 'At the end of that year, I was offered the coaching position at Norths and again,

I had a talk to Cliff about coming to Sydney. I told him that I would look after him and this time he seemed happy to come along and trial for a contract.'

In January 1985 Cliff Lyons ventured back to the city to trial for a contract with North Sydney. Gundagai team-mate Brian Dennis, a strong-running, goal-kicking centre who represented Country the previous year, also went with him. Hawick remembers, 'I told Cliff that under no circumstances was he too push himself or promote himself as something he wasn't. I told him to let his football sell himself, "Once they see what you can do, you'll be right". Cliff stood out from the pack right from the word go. He could play any position in the backline "off a break". He was head and shoulders above any player at the club.'

Lyons wasted little time in impressing Norths officials. Playing in his favoured five-eighth position in a trial against Taree, the 23-year-old rose above the atrocious playing conditions to star in the 10-all draw with the southern Group 3 team. The Bears' captain Mark Graham, who was appointed coach of the Auckland Warriors in 1999, missed the trial because of a shoulder injury but instantly picked out the stocky pivot as a player of the future. "Sydney-siders haven't a clue who this bloke is but I'll bet they will after five or six weeks," Graham told *The Mosman Daily*. "He looked terrific up in Taree, bowling over front rowers with ease and then sneaking out wide to deck other unsuspecting runners. Cliff also looks to have pretty slick ball skills and a good football brain. If I'm any sort of judge at all, Norths are on to a really good player."

Greg Hawick was quick to sing Lyons' praise to Norths. 'His durability was an important factor,' he recalls. 'I said to North Sydney that here was a player who is very durable and would be able play for a long time. He's just so strong.' Brian Dennis was first to gain a contract with Norths but Cliff's defence and his all-round ability with the ball earned him a modest, one-year incentive contract valued at \$4,000. This caused a dilemma for Cliff and his fiancée Karen. Following the forced retirement of clubman Steve Evans, Lyons was being groomed as the new captain-coach of the Gundagai Tigers.

'Clifford and Karen came around to see me,' remembers Cliff's mother who was now living in the inner city at Waterloo. 'The Bears had offered him a contract and he wanted to know what he should do because it was worth more money to return to Gundagai. I told him that it was his decision but if it was me, I would play first grade in Sydney for nothing just to get in there because I knew how difficult it was.'

Despite being over-looked for representation for Country Firsts or Seconds during his three years in the bush, Cliff had grown in confidence in his own ability and was ready to try his hand in Sydney. He now had something to play for - a future. For Cliff and Karen, the promise of a career as a professional rugby league player would see them relocate in Sydney, travel the world and later start a family together.

After Cliff left the district to play for Norths, editor Pat Sullivan lamented via *The Gundagai Independent*, 'How come, in his days with the bush, (Cliff's) ability went unrecognised by the CRL selection panel? We knew he was outstanding – all the blokes down at the pub knew he was a champion, little old ladies gossiping at the butcher's shop knew he was a potential international – but the poor, thick-headed selection panel didn't see it. In fact Cliff, in his last season with Gundagai, was not even named in the starting team for Riverina, but made it as a replacement. The CRL selection panel, over the years, has consistently refused to recognise talent.'

'It is fair to say that some people in the town thought he wouldn't make it – there were those at the football club who didn't like losing him or said that he'd be back,' says Connie Luff. 'Even at age 28 the press was saying that Cliff was getting long in the tooth. He's proven everyone wrong.' But for most, Gundagai adopted Cliff as its own with the majority of the town taking a keen interest in his future. 'A lot of local people in the town who aren't even rugby league followers started following his career,' says Connie. 'People used to send me press clippings of Cliff's matches and then friends started taping the games for us. We didn't even have a video when Cliff started playing, but I've managed to keep a copy of most of the matches he played on TV. It's something that I thought he would enjoy to keep for his children.'

'On the Monday morning after we'd been up to Sydney to watch him play,' Kevin adds, 'people would ask you in the street, "How did Cliffy go?" They'd want to know before they even read it in the papers.'

The departure of Cliff Lyons left a gaping hole in the local Group 9 competition and particularly in the Gundagai team. While the Tigers failed to make the semi finals in 1985, Lyons quickly cemented a first grade place during one of the most troubled and dramatic seasons in the long history of the North Sydney Bears.

CHAPTER THREE

North Sydney

In the twenty-five years since former South Sydney and Australian Test pivot Greg Hawick captain-coached the Bears, the world of rugby league had changed markedly. The code had evolved from the traditional, 'bash and barge' game of unlimited tackle in the early 1960s into a faster, more enterprising game under four-tackle and later, six-tackle rules. Couple this with the development of training techniques adapted from American gridiron pioneered by Jack Gibson at Easts in the mid 1970s, and Hawick faced an uphill battle to deliver the style of play North Sydney needed to be a competitive force in the game.

By the middle of the 1980s rugby league was in serious danger of becoming a stereotyped defensive contest, comprising of a number hit-ups before the predictable kick (usually a 'bomb') on the last tackle. In the 1984 grand final, the Warren Ryan-coached Canterbury team brought the free-flowing style of the superbly drilled Parramatta Eels to a close by exploiting the five-metre defensive rule with a smothering 'umbrella defence'. When North Sydney, under the guidance of former Manly premiership-winning coach Ron Willey, attempted to follow this defensive trend, club secretary Ken

McCaffrey acted swiftly. Despite the fact that Willey had taken the Bears to the semi-finals in 1982, McCaffrey felt that he personally owed Norths fans something better and sacked Willey, his friend and former 1952-53 Kangaroo team-mate.

'Talented and skilful players are now being met by a style of coaching that prevents them from developing those skills,' McCaffrey told respected rugby league writer Ian Heads in 1985. 'We're hopeful that we can be responsible for developing old thoughts on the game, and make it more enjoyable for the spectator – and the player.' Fortunately, this was exactly the philosophy that enabled a naturally gifted player like Cliff Lyons to display his raw ability in a period when most attacking players were being shackled by coaches' restrictive and conservative game plans.

McCaffrey looked to Greg Hawick, who also toured with the 1952-53 Kangaroos, to return the club to the era of open rugby league that would bring Bears fans back to the newly renovated North Sydney Oval. Hawick accepted the challenge by instituting a rigid training regime designed to improve the fitness of the players. However, many players thought Hawick's ideas outdated and narrow-minded which immediately brought him into conflict with the club's senior players.

Today Greg Hawick is reticent to go into the details of his time with the club, preferring to 'let bygones be bygones'. All he would say was that opposition to his style of coaching was there from the start and it proved an impossible hurdle to overcome. One of the few players who did not object to his coach's demands was Cliff Lyons. He quickly shed a stone from his country playing weight and was running around at a trim 83 kilograms (13 stone). Lyons says diplomatically, 'I though Greg had a lot of good ideas and was hardly done-by at Norths. I saw nothing wrong with his methods.'

While Brian Dennis was selected in the centres in the opening match of the season, Cliff started the year in reserve grade after former Wallaby international Mitchell Cox retained the five-eighth role. 'Although I had played well in the trials, I was still settling in at the club so realistically, I set myself the goal of trying to make first grade by the end of the first round of competition,' Cliff remembers. Ironically, Lyons was employed at Cox's Bowlgowlah Holden dealership as a car detailer but soon, was to take over his boss' job on the playing field.

When the Bears opened the season with a disappointing 26-6 loss to Balmain, Hawick promptly sacked five players and replaced Mark Graham as captain. Graham, a seasoned Kiwi Test forward and one of the toughest competitors in international rugby league, was replaced as captain by rookie hooker Wayne Honeywood. (Graham was later found to have played the opening matches of the season with an undiagnosed, perforated eardrum.) Mitchell Cox, who was recovering from a bout of hepatitis and was said to be lacking match condition, and former Newcastle and NSW representative hooker Rex Wright, were among those dropped.

Brian Dennis, who had scored Norths' only goal in the opening match of the season, later injured his knee, ruling him out for the season. In a cruel twist of fate, this was to be his only first grade appearance and proved to be the last in his Sydney career. Conversely, despite a mixed performance in reserve grade, Cliff Lyons was selected to make his first grade debut at five-eighth in the second game of the season against Illawarra at Wollongong Sports Ground on March 24, 1985. In a bold move by Hawick, in which he put his job on the line to get the team he wanted, Norths not only rediscovered winning form but also uncovered a budding champion in the process.

'Unheralded five-eighth Cliff Lyons was North Sydney's scene-stealer in the Bears' exciting 15-10 Winfield Cup win over Illawarra last Sunday,' wrote *The Mirror's* Tim Prentice in his report of the match. 'Lyons, 23, made a magical first grade debut, engineering all three Norths' tries and snapping a field goal for good measure.' After a nervous start to the match, Lyons set up tries for Nigel Tait, Andrew Simons and Mark Graham and gave good service to his outside backs. Similarly impressive was Lyons' defensive game in topping the tackle count and his ability to read ahead of the play. A series of jarring tackles rattled the Steeler forwards while Cliff's second-half field goal set up a winning 15-4 lead. There were jokes all round after the morale-boosting win, with Mitchell Cox threatening Lyons with overtime in the coming weeks. The signs were not encouraging for Cox making a quick return to the club's first grade line-up.

When the club went through a form slump in the middle of the season, Hawick increased the number of training sessions per week. While Hawick had the backing of club secretary Ken McCaffrey, he was quickly losing the respect of his senior players. On Sunday, April 14, Norths took on four-time grand finalists Parramatta to mark the reopening of North Sydney Oval. In the week leading up to the match the Bears' camp was rocked by the premature resignation of Mark Graham. Worn down by the constant bickering with North Sydney over the terms of his contract and unhappy with Hawick's handling of the team, Graham stood down from the match in order to overcome a recurring shoulder injury.

Norths were pipped 8-6 by the Eels in a tight match, the Bears' sole try coming from a brilliantly executed set-piece from Cliff. After winning the ball from a scrum some thirty metres from the Parramatta try-line, Lyons kicked ahead for his winger Larry Kelly to regather and dive over in the corner. It was a spectacular move – a perfect example of Lyons' confidence with the ball, but it was wasn't enough to win the match. The Bears lost because of poor fundamentals – dropped balls, missed tackles and wayward goal-kicking, while Mark Graham's no-show certainly didn't help.

Graham returned to the club for a nail-biting 18-14 win over

Souths the following week. It was widely reported that the best thing about the win was the creativity of Cliff Lyons in setting up the winning try for Paul McCaffrey. Peter Frilingos, Chief League Writer with *The Mirror*, wrote after the match, 'Like every other reporter, I wanted to interview him after the game but just before I got to him in the dressing room, I was grabbed from behind.

'Listen mate, "Rocky will play for Australia and don't forget where you heard it first," the voice behind the arm said. And while that voice belongs to one of his brothers, that prediction is looking good.' Colin Lyons had certainly made his point!

Peter Frilingos found a naturally confident and surprisingly under-whelmed Cliff Lyons taking success in his stride. 'My play hasn't changed all that much from the way I played in Gundagai,' Lyons told him after the Souths win. 'Luckily for me, Greg Hawick also believed I would make it in Sydney so I have to thank him for giving me the chance at Norths.'

'That was the day Cliff was really noticed for what he could do,' remembers Colin Lyons. 'We had a sign on the hill, *"Go Rocky! Show them the way!"* At that time there was a car add and that was the slogan so we used that. We were so excited that Norths won. I think we were all on TV because we were jumping up and down on the hill after the win.'

Three weeks later, in the 22-20 win over Wests, Cliff proved his versatility when he was handed the goal-kicking duties and successfully shifted to the centres to accommodate the return of Mitchell Cox. Although he had kicked sporadically during his career in the bush, Lyons proved himself in the muddy conditions by kicking the winning goal from the sideline. While Norths slumped to lose seven of its next eight matches, Lyons maintained his consistency while many of his more high-profile team-mates struggled in a losing team.

On the Sunday night following the win over Wests, Lyons and

team-mate Steve Hanson were informed of their selection for City Seconds. Despite again being selected on the bench, Cliff had won representative honours after just eight first grade appearances. In what can be only seen as poor management on Norths' part, the club did not inform the two rookies that the medical was on the next day. Cliff and Steve assumed that the medical and first training session would be on the following Tuesday, the usual date for club training after a weekend match. Lyons eventually arrived two hours late for the Monday morning medical while Hanson missed the session altogether and had to be passed fit the following day.

While the experienced Terry Lamb got the nod over the rookie pivot in City Seconds, Lyons made the most of his opportunities from the bench sitting alongside another young star, Penrith's Greg Alexander. Once on the field, Lyons laid on a try for Penrith centre Brad Izzard when he sent Alexander through a gap with a deftly-timed pass. Although enjoying only a brief taste of representative duty, Lyons relished the opportunity to play with the game's best players. Under the terms of his contract, he picked up a tidy $500 bonus for representing City and his continued good press saw him garner attention from several other clubs – especially when it became known that he was not under contract the following year. While Lyons felt a loyalty to both Greg Hawick and to Norths for giving him a start in the Sydney premiership, the constant phone calls from rival clubs and the uncertainty over Hawick's future with the Bears saw him put his future in the hands of manager Richard Fisk.

The situation inside the volatile Norths camp finally came to a head when Greg Hawick publicly questioned the ability of his forward pack following the 16-8 loss to Canterbury. He then seemed to sow the seeds of further discontent when he chose to ignore the match-winning return to form by Mark Graham in the club's 14-10 win over Easts the following week. As Norths spiralled to the bottom of the table in a mid-season slump, Mitchell Cox chose *Rugby League*

Week to return serve and criticise Hawick's ability as coach, describing the team's form as 'embarrassing and degrading'.

There was certainly no denying the whole-heartedness of Cliff Lyons who never gave less than what his coach expected. In the 29-6 loss to Balmain, Lyons scored all his side's points with a try and goal. For the return encounter with Illawarra, Hawick moved Lyons to lock (his third positional move in as many weeks) and named him captain. Lyons was again the club's sole try-scorer in the 26-8 loss to the Steelers, a match that drew a home crowd of just over 2000. Highlighting the fickle nature of professional rugby league, Lyons was replaced as captain for the following match.

The 42-12 loss to Canberra in front of a paltry North Sydney crowd of 1,408 spectators was the absolute nadir of a wretched season for the Bears. Those Norths fans who braved the match witnessed the demoralising sight of players abusing each other behind their own goal-posts as the fledgling Raiders, who had not won a match at the oval since the club's promotion in 1982, ran in seven tries. Ken McCaffrey, who had sacked coach Ron Willey as a protest against the style of play that he had instilled in the club, finally asked Hawick, his friend of thirty years, to stand down for the good of the team.

'Greg Hawick is a perfect gentleman,' McCaffrey told *The Mosman Daily*, 'but coaching in Sydney is a pretty cutthroat game and we have a responsibility to the club and the supporters. We set Greg a pretty formidable task to coach the side after 25 years out of the Sydney scene and obviously things have not worked out how we would have liked.' Finally acknowledging that there had been a problem between the coach and the players, McCaffrey would suffer a similar fate at season's end and was voted out of office as Club Secretary.

Hawick was replaced by reserve grade coach Brian 'Chicka' Norton, who not only had to get the Bears winning again but also had the difficult task of rebuilding team morale. The Bears started the fightback with an improved showing against Parramatta, losing 18-10, before recording a much-needed 12-8 win over Souths. The next match however, a 22-all draw with semi-final bound Penrith, was an opportunity lost for Norths and a lesson hard-learned for Cliff. Norths were holding a slender 22-20 lead with minutes remaining when visiting British referee Robin Whitfield penalised Lyons after a scrum win to Penrith. This indiscretion gave Penrith halfback Greg Alexander the opportunity to tie the match and deny Norths a much-needed victory.

While North Sydney won only one of its remaining five matches of the year, the club somehow avoided the wooden spoon to finish eleventh of thirteen teams. Lyons' continued good form made him the most sought after rookie in the game. Warren Ryan pointed him out for special praise after Canterbury's 32-14 win but Lyons refused to confirm his intentions for the following year, preferring to honour his commitments to Norths until the end of the season. It was clear though that Lyons was a player of the future who could now command in excess of ten-times what he was being paid at Norths.

Midway through the season, Lyons accepted an offer to play in England for Leeds during the 1985-86 off-season, a move not so much to capitalise on his newfound status as a marketable professional rugby league player but more an opportunity for Cliff and Karen to travel overseas. Easts and Manly lined up against Norths to battle over Lyons' future but when St George's attempt to lure Steve Ella from Parramatta failed, it was thought that the Dragons would outbid Manly for Lyons' services. However, one thing was clear. After Greg Hawick left the club, Cliff's chances of staying with the Bears grew remote. 'I was just sick of the bitching and in-fighting at the club and was not happy with the way the players or the club treated Greg,' Lyons recalls. 'I was grateful that

A budding champion - playing for
the Tregear Foxes, Under 12s

Playing for Gymeah in the Cronulla
Junior Rugby League

Brothers in arms - playing for a Koori representative team in 1983.
From left - a former brother in law, younger brother Colin, Cliff Lyons
and older brother Rick

Karen Lyons with new-born son Mathew – born the night Australia retained the Ashes, November 1990. (Courtesy Manly Daily)

(Courtesy Manly Daily)

Cliff with children Mathew and Courtney, 1994. Celebrating his 33rd birthday in hospital recovering from a hernia operation.

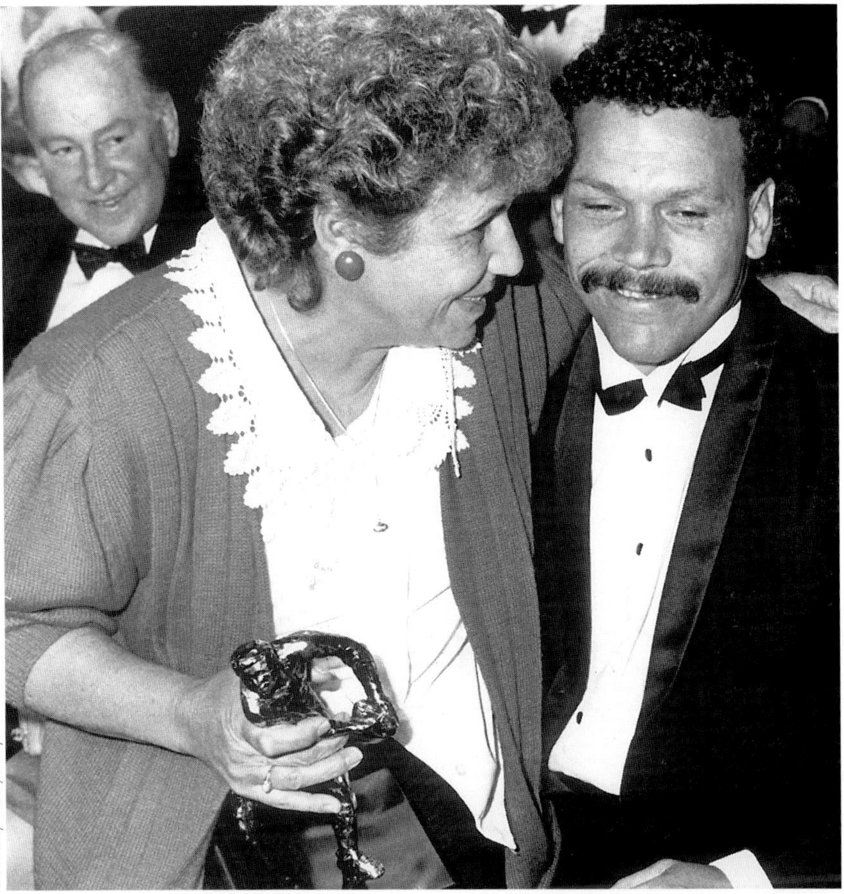

(Courtesy Manly Daily)

Cliff with mother Melva, celebrates his Gold 'Dally M' Award in 1990. Manly Chief Executive Doug Daley looks on.

(Courtesy Manly Daily)

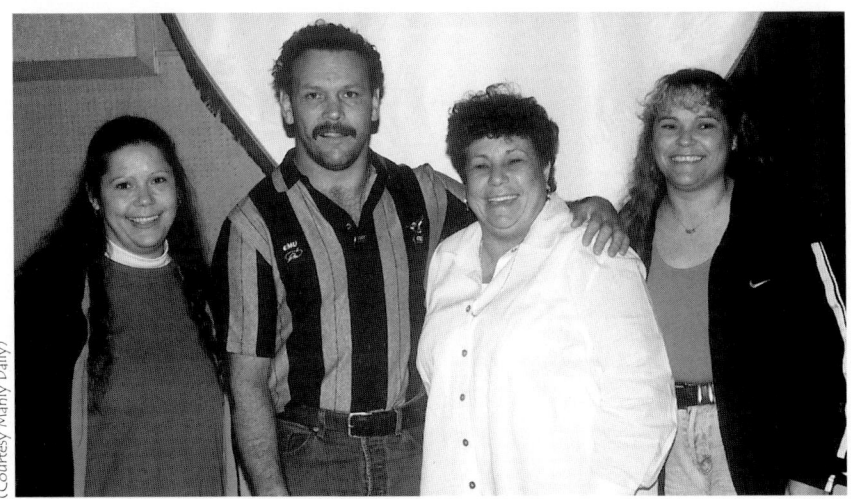

Cliff with sister Naralle, mother Melva and sister Nita, on the night of his first retirement, 1998.

With Tina Turner in London
in 1989 ...
'What you get is what you see ...'

(Courtesy Manly Daily)

Role models for a new generation - Cathy Freeman and Cliff Lyons.

Cliff, intent on giving something back to the Aboriginal community with NASCA.

(Courtesy Manly Daily)

Cliff Lyons... from 'the Bush'...

(Courtesy Manly Daily)

... to Brookvale.

At Leeds, 1988-89....displaying all
the necessary skills.

the Bears had given me a chance but I wasn't confident that they would look after me in the long term.'

Greg Hawick was also concerned. 'I wanted a club that would look after Cliff, help him to make some money and invest it safely. I wanted Cliff to go to a club that would treat him right – a move that would be to his benefit. I knew he had the talent to earn a good living. I suggested to Cliff that Manly might be that club but it was Cliff again who sold himself with his talent and quiet manner.'

Ken Arthurson, former Manly Chief Executive and then ARL Executive Chairman, takes up the story. 'I was closely connected to the decision by virtue of the fact that Roy Bull and I were friends of Greg Hawick. Greg told Roy Bull and myself that Cliff was not totally happy at North Sydney because of the problems that they were having and that he suggested that Cliff Lyons might like to play for Manly. I had admired Cliff Lyons as a player prior to that; I thought he was a great talent. We spoke to Doug Daley who was Chief Executive of the club at that time and it was Doug who made the necessary and appropriate arrangements. The impression I got was that Norths weren't particularly concerned about Cliff going because they had Mitchell Cox.'

However, Cliff's manager Richard Fisk was negotiating with Easts' coach Arthur Beetson and had come to an agreement on terms. When Cliff informed Fisk that he had a verbal contract to play with Manly in 1986, Fisk was annoyed and told Beetson that Lyons didn't want to play with Easts. Unbeknown to Cliff, Fisk was also negotiating with Manly on behalf of another of his clients – Cliff's team-mate, Mitchell Cox.

Ultimately, Cliff declined to sign with Easts, despite the enormous regard he had for Beetson. ARL Executive Chairman Ken Arthurson was also to soon discover that Cliff was difficult to move once he had committed to an agreement. 'Ken talked to Cliff about not going to England because selectors had him penciled in for the

President's XIII's tour of Papua-New Guinea,' remembers Karen Lyons. 'Cliff had a verbal agreement to play in Leeds and for the pair of us, going to England was not just about playing football. Cliff declined Ken's offer, but at the time we were concerned that this decision might affect Cliff's future chances of a 'rep' career - but it didn't.'

On September 4, one week after he finished his rookie season with North Sydney, Cliff Lyons signed with Manly-Warringah. For Sea Eagles coach Bob Fulton, it was part of a concerted rebuilding program by the club. 'Manly had finished runners-up in 1982-83 and we knew that we had to sign some new players in order to play the style of football needed in order to win the premiership. The signing of Cliff Lyons at the end of 1985 was another important piece of the jigsaw.'

It was a move that pleased all the members of his family. 'When Cliff went to Manly, I was the happiest bloke in Australia,' says Colin Lyons. 'As kids, Cliff used to go for Canterbury while (older brother) Rick was a Parramatta supporter but I was always a Manly fan.' Then he added, 'However, when I was playing in the Cronulla juniors with Cliff, it was a sin to even mention Manly.'

'The move to Manly made me really, really happy,' says Melva. 'I wasn't happy with the treatment he was getting at Norths but when he signed with Manly, club secretary Doug Daley rang me personally and congratulated me on what a fine son Clifford was. He promised that Manly would look after him and that if there was anything that the club could do for me or my family, not to hesitate to ask. He was true to his word. The first time I went over to the club, he took me around and introduced me to everyone. Whenever Clifford played, even if it was out of Sydney, he always made sure that the family had seats.'

For Karen and Cliff, it was the beginning of building their life together, first at Queenscliff and later at Dee Why. 'On the Manly peninsula, it's like our own little community,' says Karen. 'Coming from the country as we did, to us Manly was a nice little area that felt like 'home'. Now, we feel like locals – the kids go to the local school, a lot of our friends are here – people we have met through Cliff's career and those who don't have anything to do with football. It would have been easy for us to get up and leave at certain times during Cliff's career, but the only real issue for Cliff was to play for a strong club that allowed him to play the way that he wanted to play. And that may not have happened any other place other than Manly.'

At Manly-Warringah, it was a union that was to last 15 seasons.

CHAPTER FOUR

Manly-Warringah

Just before he left for England to play with Leeds, Cliff Lyons was told that the Sea Eagles had also snared his Norths team-mate Mitchell Cox for the 1986 season. At the time, Manly's signing of Cox hit Cliff like a smack on the jaw. 'It was a shock at the time,' says Cliff, 'Norths seemed more keen to retain Mitchell than me and so I left for Manly. I battled all year to hold the first grade five-eighth position and now I had to do it all over again. It was both good and bad in a way.'

While realising that signing with Manly did not guarantee an armchair ride into first grade, the fact that Manly now had four top class halves - Des Hasler, Phil Blake, Mitchell Cox and himself, made the situation extremely competitive. Manly allowed Lyons to miss the opening matches of the 1986 season but in the back of his mind all through that winter in England was the nagging worry that Mitchell Cox would have five weeks head-start in cementing the first grade five-eighth position.

Leeds, situated in the north of England and surrounded by the rugby league strongholds of Bradford, Castleford, Wakefield and Halifax, is about as far away from Gundagai as you can get. With its headquarters at Headingly, Cliff found himself playing at the acknowledged home of English rugby league in arguably the finest stadium in England.

Lyons continued a long line of Australian players to play with Leeds including Eric Harris, Arthur Clues, Keith McLellan and Ken and Dick Thornet.

'When we arrived we were jet-lagged and nervous that we may have made the wrong decision to come to England,' recalls Karen. 'We were taken straight to Headingly to have publicity photos taken and Cliff played the next day!' Coached by former Great Britain international halfback Peter Fox, Lyons made an immediate impression when he crossed for three tries in a blistering eight-minute period in the 60-21 thrashing of Keighley. Karen recalls, 'The Leeds supporters broke into song, singing 'Waltzing Matilda' after Cliff had scored, and I knew we had made the right decision.'

'I felt very tired in the first half but picked up later,' Lyons told Manchester reporter Jack McNamara. Cliff found it difficult at first because he didn't know the names of his team-mates but a more pressing problem plagued his stay in England – he could not understand the thick Yorkshire accent of the locals. They, on the other hand, had little trouble with Cliff because he didn't say much anyway. Lyons also had trouble fitting into the traditional English mould of pivot, which is predominantly to feed the ball to the outside backs. After a couple of games, he moved to the centres and was allowed more freedom to run with the ball but following suspensions to the club's regular halfbacks, Lyons moved to halfback despite having had limited experience behind the scrumbase.

'The English game has too much 'one-out' play,' Cliff recalls. 'At five-eighth, I used to yell for the ball but they wouldn't pass it. I played the last 12 games at Leeds at halfback and that's when I really hit my straps. But it took me a while to learn all the tricks.' An early highlight of Cliff's time at Leeds was the 21-8 win over St Helens in which Lyons set up two tries and landed a mammoth 45-yard field goal.

Australian players dominated English rugby league in the winter of 1985-86. Chris Anderson captain-coached Halifax – a side that contained his former Canterbury team-mates Darryl Brohman and Geoff Robinson; Geoff Gerard, John Dorahy, Peter Johnston and Gavin Miller were at Hull KR, Neil Baker and Mick Pobjie at Salford, while a broken leg in his opening match for Widnes against Wigan ended the career of legendary Test centre Steve Rogers. Lyons was joined by young Brisbane centre Tony Currie, another budding Test player who, having already tasted State of Origin success, was moving to Sydney to play with Canterbury in 1986.

During his time in England Cliff's playing weight had ballooned out to 92 kgs (14.5 stone), the result of a hamstring injury that sidelined him for six matches, poor training methods and huge quantities of fish and chips. 'We played in the snow,' Cliff said on his return. 'It was the first time I had seen the stuff. It cut your knees like razor blades. And the fans threw snowballs!' The match against Halifax was twice cancelled because of the snow on the field. 'The local radio asked supporters to get down to the field with shovels and clear the ground if they wanted the game to go ahead,' remembers Karen, who had been joined by her parents, her brother and his wife and later Cliff's mother, Melva. 'When we arrived at the ground there were huge mounds of snow behind each goal post. Three-hundred fans had worked all day to make the ground playable.'

As Leeds charged into the semi-finals of the Challenge Cup, Lyons drew desperately close to the March 31 deadline that dictated that Australian players could not play in international matches unless they intended to stay for the rest of the season. In the semi-final against Hull KR, the Rovers trailed 12-2 after half-back Paul Harkin was sent off for tripping Tony Currie. Inspired by its Australian contingent, Hull fought back to lead 24-14 with John Dorahy setting up two tries and landing two goals. Late in the match, Leeds snatched a thrilling 24-all draw to force a replay on the following Thursday.

With Cliff due to fly home after the match against Bradford Northern the following day, Leeds officials lamented the thought of its Australian stars missing the replay the following week. 'We hope the Australian authorities will be sympathetic for what is an important cup tie for the both the club and the players,' said Leeds chairman Harry Jepson. The club then announced that it was seeking permission from Australian authorities for Lyons and Currie to delay their departure and stay past the March 31 deadline. Surprisingly, Manly, a club that had taken the gamble and invested in Cliff's future, allowed him to stay an extra week. 'We agreed to Lyons staying on because it's such a big occasion for him,' Doug Daley said in defending the decision.

When Melva Kennedy remarked that she would miss the final if Leeds won the replay because her holiday was ending, Jepson told her not to worry. 'If Leeds makes the final,' Melva remembers him saying, 'we'll fly you and Cliff back to England on the Concorde!' When questioned about Lyons' availability if Leeds won the semi-final and made the Wembley final, Doug Daley was a little more guarded. 'That decision will be made later on and will depend on Manly's playing strength at the time,' Daley said.

Unfortunately, Leeds was beaten by Hull in the semi-final replay the following Thursday and Lyons immediately flew home to train with Manly. There was no joy for Hull's Australian players either, losing to the Mal Reilly-coached Castleford in the Cup Final in front of 100,000 fans. Before he left, Lyons rejected an offer to return to Leeds to concentrate on his first season with Manly. Having proven himself in England, he now set his sights on every first grade player's dream - the Kangaroo Tour at season's end.

'People may think I'm crazy for knocking back such a big offer but I have other priorities,' Cliff told *The Mirror's* Tony Adams on his return. 'Manly has been good to me, allowing me to stay in England as long as possible – and I want to get into their top side.' Lyons returned to Sydney on the first weekend in April, with six rounds of competition completed and Mitchell Cox in superb form at five-eighth.

Manly coach Bob Fulton publicly stated that he intended easing Cliff Lyons back into the Sydney premiership in reserve grade against Cronulla. After the highs of English club football, it would have been easy for Cliff to 'turn it up' for his new club, playing well below his ability, but that is not in his nature. He immediately impressed the club's two former champion five-eighths, reserve grade coach Alan Thompson and first grade mentor Bob Fulton, who remarked that Cliff 'oozed class' and was impressed by Lyons' strength and adaptability.

'He's a class player. Nothing less,' Fulton told the *Daily Telegraph's* Grantlee Kieza. 'He has that same quality that marks other great players in the fact that he has so much time up his sleeve. He's one pass ahead of the play all the time. There aren't too many players with his football brain.'

It didn't take long for Cliff to endear himself to his new team-mates and to his coach. 'Cliff has always had an ordinary looking *"melon"*,' says Bob Fulton jokingly. 'He always appeared to have a large head and his curly hair just made it stand out more. I called him *'Napper'* one day at training - it's just a slang term for head. "Have a look at your 'Napper'!" I said to him and the other players latched on to it. The name certainly stuck.'

Cliff was quickly regaining his fitness but Fulton resisted the temptation to rush him back into first grade in the centres against lowly ranked Wests in the next match, preferring to use him from the bench. In the subsequent wash-up after the upset loss to the Magpies, former Queensland international Chris Close was dropped, Noel Cleal was switched to the centres, Paul Vautin moved to the second row with Cliff promoted to lock. Lyons was quickly proving his versatility – a five-eighth with Norths, centre and halfback with Leeds and lock at Manly - a situation that would not have been lost on the national selectors.

Cliff made his debut in Manly's first grade starting line-up in the match against Penrith at Brookvale Oval on April 27, 1986. Manly won the match 16-10 but Lyons showed his rashness when he was sin-binned for ten-minutes for tripping opposing half Greg Alexander as the two contested the ball. It was an early indication of an aggressive style that was creeping into Cliff's play – a style that threatened to tarnish his reputation as a classy ball-player. Paul Vautin suffered a broken arm in the match, an injury that would see him out of the game for the next four months and paved the way for Cliff to secure the lock position for much of the season.

'As a lock forward, Cliff certainly didn't have the skills of the guy he was replacing but it was important that he was in the side somewhere,' says Bob Fulton. On the following Wednesday, in a midweek cup match against St George at Newcastle Sports Centre, Manly hammered the previous season's grand finalists, 18-2, with the continued good form of half-back partnership Hasler and Cox a highlight of the match. Lyons made up for giving away two early penalties to score the first try of the match after St George fullback Glen Burgess spilled a bomb and Lyons was on hand to pounce on the ball.

After the victory against St George, Manly thrashed Easts 30-24, while Lyons and Cox would have gained immense satisfaction from the 28-24 win over their former club Norths in the next round.

The 8-4 loss to Souths the following week did not reflect the resolute courage the injury-plagued Manly side showed in the face of a fired up Rabbitohs team. Lyons was again sin-binned, along with three other players, after an all-in brawl but he had been injured in the first tackle of the match and hobbled around the field until eventually replaced early in the second half.

Cliff retained the lock position as Manly bounced back with an authoritative 30-18 win over Parramatta. Lyons then opened the scoring in the match against Canberra with a field goal in the ninth minute and backed this up with a try as Manly surged to a 25-18 win in a see-sawing match at Seiffert Oval. Lyons scored two tries as Manly thrashed St George 52-20 in a match that marked the return to form of Phil Blake who was deputising at halfback for the injured Des Hasler. The Manly team was receiving rave reviews for the manner in which it was winning matches – resolute toughness and exciting tries, but gained the wrong sort of press the following week in the match against Balmain.

On Monday, June 30, 1986, the Sydney public awoke to the sight of photos of Cliff Lyons clashing with rival Balmain forward Mike Marketo splashed over the front page of the *Daily Telegraph*. The three photos, captioned 'Bunch, Punch, Crunch!' showed Lyons landing a 'full-blown punch of which Jeff Fenech would have been proud'. Manly lost a tough Leichhardt Oval encounter, 14-9, with Cliff wrongly being portrayed in the press as the club's resident hothead.

'Cliff was a marked man if he didn't stand up for himself and I doubt his career would have lasted as long as it did had he not defended himself,' says Karen Lyons who had grown increasingly angry at the manner in which rival players were targeting Cliff. 'The Balmain forward in question shadowed Cliff for the entire game and never let up. I felt he wasn't getting a lot of protection from referees and lineman at the time. Cliff simply had enough.'

Cliff slotted back into the role of five-eighth for the match against Illawarra following the withdrawal of Mitchell Cox. Manly won the match 14-12 after a penalty try was awarded to Manly hooker Mal Cochrane by rookie referee Bill Harrigan. Lyons produced a key defensive effort against the unlucky Steelers, moving Bob Fulton to write in his *Daily Mirror* column, 'Few players can put a player into a gap like Lyons does and he has the ability to chip and line kick and defend strongly for 80 minutes. Throw in an amazing desire to win every game he plays and you have a footballer who would be an enormous asset on the Kangaroo Tour.'

'Bob had a couple of goes at changing me but I think he realized all the fitness work and weight training in the world couldn't change what I could do,' says Cliff. 'I have always been naturally fit but there has been this myth about me that I was not a great trainer. Maybe I just made it look easy. I enjoyed training - I did it willingly. I didn't do much weight work because I was naturally strong.'

Cliff underlined this opinion in the next game. Shifted to lock following the withdrawal of key players Mitchell Cox and Dale Shearer, Lyons topped the tackle count, making 27 tackles in the 32-4 thrashing of Cronulla. Cliff again topped the tackle count in the match against Wests the following week but for the second time that year, Wests defeated Manly 22-20 in a major upset. Sea Eagles' captain Noel Cleal, backing up after the Second Test against New Zealand which was played the day before, was replaced just after half-time with Cliff moving to second-row and taking on the lion's share of the tackling in the loss to the Magpies.

Lyons was quickly being hailed as the 'buy of the year' but the absence of a playmaker behind the scrumbase was hurting the Sea Eagles in the run-up to the semi-finals. Following an 11-all draw with Penrith, Manly was pipped 24-22 by Easts and then beaten 14-8 by Norths. Lyons was regularly topping the tackle count but his new-found defensive role was also dulling his attack. The club returned to form in the 16-8 win over defending premiers Canterbury with Lyons crossing for the try to seal the match.

Despite the fact that Cliff's late return to Australia had cost him a place in the early season representative matches, his continued good form and versatility saw him press for Kangaroo selection. Former Manly and Australian Test captain Max Krilich joined the growing chorus calling for Lyons' name to be added to the Kangaroo Tourists when he wrote, 'If there is a better or more valuable utility player in the game then I haven't seen him. To play the way he did against a pack like Canterbury last Sunday was nothing short of sensational.'

In spite of its late season slump, Manly was still in sight of the minor premiership with two matches remaining but losses to Parramatta (22-8) and Souths (23-18) saw the Sea Eagles finish in fourth place in the final five. Manly had a disastrous time with injuries with Rothmans medal winner Mal Cochrane ruled unavailable for the sudden death semi-final match against Balmain. In a spirited end to one of the closest competitions on record, Balmain qualified for the semi-finals after winning a mid-week play-off for fifth spot against Norths.

The elimination semi-final against Balmain, which saw Manly crash out of the premiership race after a promising start to the season, can be viewed as the turning point in Cliff's career. After 14 minutes of play, Manly raced to a 12-0 lead but by half-time, Balmain had fought its way back to a 19-12 advantage. The Tiger forwards, led by Steve Roach and Paul Sironen, unsettled the Manly pack with some torrid defence and the first half had erupted in several vicious incidents, a flow-over of ill-feeling from the second round clash at Leichhardt Oval.

Early in the second half, with Manly struggling to stay in the match, the Sea Eagles were dealt a deathblow for the season when Lyons was dismissed by referee Kevin Roberts. Balmain led 25-22 against a courageous 12-man Manly team in the final stages of the match before a late try sealed a 29-22 victory. Lyons faced the judiciary on a charge of 'kneeing another player to the head after a previous caution for using a knee'. Manly Chief Executive Doug Daley argued that Cliff's knee did not come into contact with the head of Balmain halfback Scott Gale but rather the shoulder area. However, Daley admitted that Lyons had over-reacted to sledging from the Balmain players.

'Lyons was submitted to a lot of that sledging while a Balmain player had hit him (Lyons) twice in that tackle and plenty had been said,' Daley told the judiciary. When questioned by Daley, referee Kevin Roberts said that he was unaware of any sledging during the game and reiterated that Lyons' knee had come into contact with the top of Gale's head. Daley sought clemency from the panel, stating that Lyons had never been sent off in a twelve-year career and he was in fact in line for a club award as the player who most contributed to the Sea Eagles' success that season.

The panel took a dim view of Daley's argument and suspended Lyons for four matches. Although he was selected for the train-on squad for the Kangaroos, Lyons had all but seen his chances of playing for his country that year disappear. Dale Shearer, Des Hasler, Paul Vautin, Noel Cleal, Phil Daley, Mal Cochrane and Cliff Lyons were added to the train-on squad but when the names of the 26 players were read out, Shearer, Cleal, Hasler and Daley were selected. While Paul Vautin, who had missed that year's representative fixtures because of his broken arm, and Mal Cochrane, a talented hooker/goal-kicker who had won the Rothmans Medal that year, can be considered very unlucky not to tour, no-one had a better case for selection than Lyons.

'No way did I knee the player in the head,' says Cliff. 'I was just trying to slow down the play the ball and leant on the player to keep him on the ground longer. The judiciary was down on the

Manly players after incidents involving Ron Gibbs and Phil Daley but there was no way I deserved to get four weeks. Realistically, I now had no chance of making the Kangaroo Tour. For the remainder of the train-on squad I was thinking that they wouldn't take me just to warm the bench for the first four matches. There was just so many good players fighting for the five-eighth position.' Undoubtedly, his suspension cost him a place on the tour. With a glut of half-backs and five-eighths on offer, selectors chose Wally Lewis (captain), Peter Sterling (vice-captain), Des Hasler, Brett Kenny and Terry Lamb. When Parramatta winger Eric Grothe was ruled out of the tour, selectors called upon Penrith halfback Greg Alexander.

Cliff was duly named 'Clubman of the Year' as the player who contributed the most to the 'success and prestige' of the club. 'Bob Fulton arranged for Cliff to go to England and play with Second Division team, the Sheffield Eagles for six weeks so that he could serve out his four-match-suspension,' says Karen Lyons. 'This move had nothing to do with money or furthering his career but simply to do what the club wanted him to do. We had decided to get married in early 1987 and there was a lot of planning to do so I didn't go with Cliff to England.'

'We thought about delaying the wedding but it would have disappointed too many people,' says Karen. 'Cliff returned to Australia a week before the wedding so it was quite good planning on his part because he missed having to make all the arrangements.' With eldest brother Ricky as his best man, Cliff married Karen Luff in March 1987. They were both 25 years of age.

CHAPTER FIVE

Grand Final Glory

Cliff Lyons' two career goals, Australian selection and a grand final lap of honour around the SCG in September with Manly, had been set back because of poor self-discipline. Maybe he wanted to prove himself *too much* - tackling harder, running faster and kicking longer than any other player, but he was also being sucked in to one-one confrontations with opponents who were using any means available to unsettle him and get on top of him.

'Cliff's always had a little bit of "mongrel" in his game,' says Bob Fulton, 'and there certainly was the case of being the "new kid on the block" at Manly and wanting to prove himself. But I never consciously tried to change his style of play. It was just a case of Cliff adjusting to what was required at the club.'

Seldom in 1987 did Cliff loose his cool but once, after being sin-binned for punching his opponent, his mother Melva again raised the issue after the match. 'I asked him what happened,' she recalls, 'and he said the other player called him an 'Aboriginal'. I think he actually called him something else but Clifford didn't want to say it. "*An Aboriginal*," I said to him. "You should have patted the guy on the head for finally being able to work it out!"'

Newly-married, Karen remembers the 1987 season for many things other than the fact that Manly won the premiership. 'There was a great feeling in the club,' Karen recalls. 'Maybe it was the fact that we all didn't have children yet, but there was a great social atmosphere at Manly. We all lived close to each other at Queenscliff in flats owned by the club and we all went out to dinner together on a regular basis. At different times over the next few years, Megan and Ronny Gibbs lived below us, Chris White and his wife Sonia lived in the same block, Michael and Susan O'Connor lived around the corner, Darrell Williams and his wife, Mark and Karen Brokenshire, Tony Iro and his wife Harriett, Greg and Karen Austin, Joe and Kim Ropati; we all socialised together. Des and Chris Hasler were also married at the end of the year, so a lot happened in 1987.'

Once again Cliff started the season at lock, with Martin Meredith and Des Hasler holding down the halfback partnership. The first game of the season marked the debut of 1986 Kangaroo Michael O'Connor, a player with whom Cliff was to form an important combination. 'Mick O'Connor is one of the best players I played with,' says Cliff. 'He was fantastic on his feet, very balanced, and gifted with the ball. He was a tremendous player.' O'Connor provided another piece of the premiership-winning 'jigsaw' Bob Fulton was looking for.

After an unsettled start to the season, Manly commenced an unbeaten run of 12 matches from April to August, the most dominant performance by a club since the Jack Gibson-coached Easts won the premiership in 1975. Manly started the season with a 4-all draw against Michael O'Connor's former club St George. Cliff was injured in the game and missed the next two matches before making his return from the bench against Parramatta. Manly trounced the defending premiers, 26-4, before losing their next three matches.

Lyons finally won the coveted five-eighth role against Souths but the dismissal of Phil Daley and Phil Blake marked a volatile match which Manly lost 28-18. The following week was the clash against Cronulla that sparked Bob Fulton's infamous quote about referee Bill Harrigan ('I hope you get run over by a cement truck!'). Manly led 12-4 at half-time and a Cliff Lyons field goal inched them ahead before a concerted Cronulla fightback. The Sea Eagles eventually crashed to lose 18-13 after Des Hasler was sin-binned late in the match for repeated scrum infringements.

The first match of the club's winning streak, against Easts, saw Lyons momentarily falter in his goal of staying on the right side of referees when he was dismissed for using a forearm in the tackle on a player on the ground. The 12-man Manly team held on to win the match, 18-10, with Lyons subsequently exonerated by the judiciary when the video replay clearly showed an Easts' player pulling Cliff down on top of him. The 18-10 win over Canberra at a cold and wet Seiffert Oval is remembered for a sickening injury to Mal Meninga. Chasing Darrell Williams who was attempting to run the ball out from inside the Manly in-goal area, Meninga tackled the Kiwi fullback but slid into the goal posts, shattering his left arm. Lyons, who was close by in support of Williams, was the first player to go to Mal's aid.

'The ground was very slippery that day and Mal stopped Darrell in a copybook tackle but his big frame slid into the goalpost,' says Cliff. 'His left arm took the full impact and you could clearly hear the break. I went over to him straight away because I knew it was broken.' It was the beginning of a horror eighteen months for the Canberra captain who suffered a further three breaks of the arm before cementing his place as one of the greatest captains in the history of the game.

In May, Lyons' representative aspirations suffered a huge blow when he was over-looked for selection in the Country-City matches. In 1987, for the first time, there were three teams selected – City Origin, City Firsts and City Seconds, but a place could not be found for Cliff in any side, even as a replacement. Manly defeated Norths 30-22 and thrashed the then competition leaders Balmain, 48-14 in a game that marked the debut of Castleford prop Kevin Ward. 'Kevin was an absolute bonus to the side,' says Cliff 'except that he talked in a thick Yorkshire accent and you couldn't understand what he was saying.' The stout Great Britain Test forward would return home for his club's domestic season before Manly took the unprecedented step of flying Ward back to Australia once the club qualified for the grand final.

Cliff turned in his best performance of the year with a dominant attacking display in the 20-8 win over St George. He then repeated the dose in the narrow 12-10 victory over Penrith before sparking a concerted fightback against Wests in the next match. Down 25-12 with 16 minutes to play, Lyons scored a try and provided the space for Manly backs Stuart Davis, Michael O'Connor and David Ronson to surge Manly to a 26-25 victory. Cliff clearly out-pointed his Parramatta opponent Brett Kenny with his try-scoring effort in the high scoring 30-22 win over the Eels. It was a standout performance that brought him right into calculation for State of Origin selection.

NSW won the first State of Origin match of the series 20-16 with a last-gasp try to Cronulla centre Mark McGaw, with selectors opting to retain the champion Parramatta halfback combination of Brett Kenny and Peter Sterling for the return match at the SCG. The Blues were beaten in heavy conditions, 12 points to 6 with NSW selectors then made ten positional changes for the deciding match of the series. In a bold gamble, selectors broke up the Kenny-Sterling partnership to find a place for Cliff Lyons at five-eighth. Kenny moved to the centres to partner Michael O'Connor while

Phil Daley, Lyons' Manly team-mate, made his debut in the NSW forward pack.

It was thought that Manly would struggle against a full-strength Canterbury side, given that Paul Vautin, Dale Shearer, Cliff Lyons and Michael O'Connor were absent on State of Origin duty and Darrell Williams was in training with the New Zealand Test team. However, the Sea Eagles confirmed their status as the team to beat with a resounding 32-2 win over the Bulldogs. In a troubled lead-up to the match, it was leaked by the press that Ron Gibbs would leave Manly at the end of the year as the newly promoted Gold Coast Giant's star signing for 1988. Fired up by local criticism of his decision to leave the club, with Manly fans demanding that Gibbs return Terry Randall's coveted No.10 jersey, Gibbs produced the game of the season to tear the Bulldogs pack apart. Cliff developed an affinity for the quiet country forward who, off the field, was nothing like his on-field persona of tackling assassin. He and Karen remain firm friends with the Gibbs' and stay with them when holidaying.

The cauldron that was Lang Park proved to be everything Cliff had heard it was - and more. There was nothing subtle about the pre-match entertainment with the parochial Queensland crowd whipped into a frenzy by the sight of a giant cockroach being subdued by a pest controller wearing Wally Lewis' No.6 maroon jersey. 'When you got out onto the field, the noise was incredible,' Cliff remembers. 'I was nervous at first and found it difficult to hear the calls from my team-mates but the crowd settled down a bit after NSW scored.'

Two incidents, both involving debutante Cliff Lyons, had a marked affect on the outcome of the series described by ARL chief Ken Arthurson as the most competitive and exciting series in the history of State of Origin. The scores were locked 8-all when Queensland referee Barry 'The Grasshopper' Gomersall awarded a questionable penalty to the Maroons. Lyons tried a chip-kick midway between the quarter and halfway mark with his Manly team-mate Michael O'Connor regathering the ball in brilliant fashion. Not only did Gomersall rule O'Connor offside, thereby denying NSW an important attacking position, but he incorrectly penalised NSW at the point where Lyons kicked the ball instead of the place where O'Connor regathered the ball. This gave Dale Shearer a much closer shot at penalty goal, which he duly landed.

The second incident involving Cliff produced one of the best tackles seen in interstate football. After excellent lead-up work from O'Connor, Kenny and Brian Johnston, Lyons found himself with what appeared to be an uninterrupted run to the try-line – and victory for NSW. However, Maroon fullback Gary Belcher had not fully committed himself to the Johnston tackle before the pass was given to Lyons. In an incredible feat of athleticism and agility, Belcher turned on the spot and gave chase to pull Lyons down five metres from the line. In desperation, Cliff threw an overhead pass to Johnston but it was ruled that the St George centre put his foot into touch after regathering the ball.

Late in the match, Lyons was replaced by Mark McGaw, with Brett Kenny shifting back to five-eighth, but the Maroons steadfastly defended its 10-8 half-time lead until the full-time siren to win its first interstate series in three years. NSW had made enough breaks to win the match but couldn't finish off a number of promising moves. Cliff took the brunt of the criticism from the Sydney press – he had tried too hard, he didn't fit in to coach, Ron Willey's plan, even that he wasn't ready for representative football. 'Just the same old stuff,' Cliff says with a shrug of the shoulders.

Cliff received some consolation when he was retained in the NSW side for the historic fourth State of Origin, which was played in Long Beach California. In a what now can be seen as a premature gamble to promote the game overseas, the ARL took its State of

Origin showpiece to Veteran's Memorial Stadium. In what was seen by most as a just reward for the 30 players who had given their all for the most memorable series on record, Lyons took his place on fog-covered field in front of a crowd of just over 12,000.

Although the match was not part of that year's series, the NSW players saw the match as an opportunity to unofficially square the series. NSW led 10-2 at half-time with Sterling and Lyons linking brilliantly with the speedy Blues backline. Andrew Ettingshausen, Mark McGaw, Michael O'Connor, Jonathan Docking and Lyons all scored tries with NSW running out comfortable winners, 30-18. While the match may have not had the same level of intensity as traditional State of Origin contests, the local American media was won over by the size of the entourage of Australian newspaper press and TV cameras following the two teams. 'That was my first trip to the States,' says Cliff of the historic sojourn to California. 'The day after the match a group of us, including NSW captain Peter Sterling, went up to Anaheim and did the Disneyland tour.'

Following the end of the representative season, the Sea Eagles suffered only two losses in the remainder of the season. It was Easts that finally ended Manly's winning run, 26-16, giving an early indication of what challenges would come to the Sea Eagles' premiership aspirations. The Sea Eagles struggled to beat Canberra 20-18, a side that had grown in confidence during the year and was bound to be boosted by the imminent return of Mal Meninga from injury.

In the final match of the premiership, Cliff masterminded the 26-8 demolition of Balmain, proving the Sea Eagles' newfound supremacy over their nemesis of just twelve months before. In the preliminary semi-finals, Souths defeated a disappointing Balmain side 15-12, while Easts accounted for Canberra 25-16. On the following Saturday, Canberra thrashed the Rabbitohs 46-14 and in the toughest match of the year, Manly edged out Easts 10-6 in the major semi-final on the Sunday.

Under the final five system, minor premiers Manly only had to win one match to qualify for the premiership decider and treated the match like a mini grand final. One of the reasons for the club's great form in 1987 was Lyons' ability to spark the talented Sea Eagles' backline. Manly scored 553 points in 1987 – 80 points more than its nearest rivals, and crossed for 95 tries. Captain Paul Vautin later recalled in a television retrospective of great grand final contests, 'That was one of the best backlines that I've ever been associated with. Hasler and Lyons as the halves, Williams and O'Connor in the centres, underrated wingers David Ronson and Stuart Davis, and Dale Shearer at fullback. Sensational!'

While Manly had two weeks to regroup after the narrow win over Easts, few of the Sea Eagles players who played in that match fancied the Roosters chances of backing up a week later against a fired-up Canberra side. Sparked by the return of Mal Meninga, who played just over 60 minutes of the match with his arm heavily bandaged, the Raiders defeated Easts 32-24, in a high-scoring game that produced ten tries. The scores were locked at 14-all at half-time but the Roosters faded in the second half, the effects of the previous week's match clearly evident.

'The following weekend (after the Easts' win),' Vautin recalled, 'we could hardly run we were that sore and sorry. Bob Fulton was such a good coach that he was able to bring us back to a peak for the grand final.' The 1987 grand final marked an important piece of rugby league history in that it was the last grand final played on the Sydney Cricket Ground. After 76 years of premiership deciders and international matches alike, the code was vacating the ground for the Sydney Football Stadium, which was to be built on the site of the old Sydney Sports Ground. This piece of history was not lost on Cliff, who used the occasion to grab a lasting momento of the day – the Clive Churchill Medal.

'I had played in grand finals before, even winning one with Gundagai, but it was nothing like what I experienced in 1987,' Cliff says. 'This was before team buses were used to take us to the match and we were told to just make our own way to the ground. I had to be at the ground early to pick up a 2GB Radio Award from Peter Peters and Greg Hartley – a new car for Player of the Year. Ron Gibbs talked Kevin Ward and me into travelling to the SCG in a stretch limousine as a surprise for our wives. We certainly arrived in style!'

Sunday, September 27, 1987. The grand final was played in unseasonable hot conditions with the middle of the SCG rock hard and bare of grass. Incredibly, Kevin Ward who arrived from England just two days before the big match, lasted the full eighty minutes in what must have seemed like heat-wave conditions. Early in the match, Manly attempted to exploit gaps out wide with Lyons skirting the edges of the ruck to link up with his outside backs while an astute kicking game from Dale Shearer kept the Raiders hemmed in on their own side of half-way. Lyons stepped inside the Raiders' defence and found Noel Cleal charging on to the ball but Cleal's final pass to Des Hasler was ruled forward. Another attacking raid broke down when Cliff's pass to Michael O'Connor went to ground.

Running from the base of a scrum win on the Canberra quarter-line, Des Hasler passed to Dale Shearer who made the extra man in the Manly backline and gave the ball to Lyons. Cliff shrugged off the tackle of Chris O'Sullivan with a magnificently-timed, left-handed fend and stepped inside Gary Belcher to score. 'Cliff was rampant in the first half,' remembers Paul Vautin, 'he really cut them to shreds. Every time he touched the ball he did something sensational.' Cliff's defence was also a highlight of the first half, taking his bigger opponents Ashley Gilbert and Brett Todd to ground with grass-cutting tackles and giving his opposing pivot Chris O'Sullivan no peace.

Leading 6-0, Michael O'Connor took Manly further ahead with a penalty conversion after the resumption of play. The Sea Eagles kept the pressure on Canberra by charging down two attempted clearing kicks by a tiring Mal Meninga. After a run by Peter Jackson, Manly's Phil Daley was penalised for a high tackle and Meninga's goal finally put Canberra on the scoreboard, 8-2.

O'Connor extended the lead to eight points with another penalty goal and when Shearer's crossfield kick was grounded over the line by the champion centre in the Paddington corner of the ground in the 57th minute, that lap of honour seemed only a formality. Although David Ronson, who shadowed O'Connor as the Manly centre grounded the ball, was clearly off-side, it was touch and go whether the try-scorer was in front of Shearer's kick. O'Connor's conversion cemented Manly's lead at 16-2.

Canberra responded with a clever try in the 70th minute to snap the Sea Eagles out of any complacency. Chris O'Sullivan went down 'injured' after being tackled and then miraculously popped up in the next passage of play to take the inside pass from Ivan Henjack and score. It was an ingeniously constructed 'mouse trap' play but also an illegal one because at that time, attacking players also had to be five metres behind the dummy half. Nevertheless, Belcher narrowed the scores to 16-8 with his conversion from beside the posts. Minutes later, in a run-around movement with O'Connor, Des Hasler was desperately unlucky not to score when he dropped the ball over the line when trying to avoid the corner post.

Just before full-time, O'Connor landed his fifth goal when the Raiders were penalised in front of their own posts. The full-time score, 18-8, was a fair indication of Manly's supremacy on the day and indeed, throughout the year. The Manly players carried their captain Paul Vautin from the field as they milled around the victory dais waiting for the presentation of trophies. 'If there was one player you'd want in the trenches beside you it would be 'Fatty' Vautin,' says Lyons emphatically. 'He was a player who always led by example and was simply inspirational that day.'

The Clive Churchill Medal, voted by the three remaining 'Immortals' named by *Rugby League Week*, is given to the best and fairest player in the grand final. With Manly coach Bob Fulton abstaining from voting, Cliff Lyons was the choice made by Reg Gasnier and John Raper. On hand to give him the award was a man who played a pivotal role in bringing Lyons to Manly. 'I felt an immense personal satisfaction because I always knew he was a great player,' says ARL Chief Ken Arthurson, 'and on that particular day, he was certainly the player of the match. He scored a great try, surging for the line, and tackled his heart out. One of his *fortes* as a player was his great strength and given how big he is, many a good player underestimated Cliff's determination and strength.'

Sitting in the grandstand that day was also Melva Kennedy and her family. 'The 1987 grand final was one of the happiest days of my life,' says Melva. 'Manly was in front for the whole match so I wasn't as stressed out as I normally was. One of the spectators sitting near us, all decked out in his Manly gear, recognised who I was and spread the word that Cliff's mother was in the stand. As soon as the game was finished and the team started their lap of honour, the fans led me down to the fence where I caught up with Clifford and gave him a big hug.'

After the match, Cliff wanted Melva to join him in the limousine back to Manly Leagues Club for the celebration dinner but mindful of her other children, she made her own way to the club and ensured that all her children were close by to enjoy the moment. '(Manly Chief Executive) Doug Daley said to me that night, "Melva, your son is an out-and-out champion." I thanked him and replied politely that I had six children and that they were all champions.'

CHAPTER SIX

Grand Final Hangover

In October 1987 Manly travelled halfway round the world to take part in the first Club Challenge on English soil. Although clearly favoured to win the match, the Sydney premiers faced an almost impossible hurdle to back-up after the end of the Australian season. While the Sea Eagles received few favours from the English referee, the club was still in celebration mode after their lap around the SCG and were beaten in a tryless match by the Graham Lowe-coached Wigan team, 8-2.

'Manly used the gate takings from the World Club challenge to fly the wives of the players and officials to Hawaii to spend a week with the team on the way home from England,' Karen Lyons recalls. 'It was a lovely gesture by the club that was much appreciated by everyone.' Playing in England also whetted Cliff's appetite for another stint of English club football and soon after, he accepted an offer to play for Leeds in the 1988-89 off-season.

With the Clive Churchill Medal sitting alongside Cliff's

premiership medallion, one other goal remained - selection for Australia. The Bicentennial year provided a host of representative opportunities with a three-Test series against the visiting Great Britain team, a one-off Test against Papua-New Guinea and a match against a specially selected 'Rest of the World' team. The 1988 season also saw the introduction of three new clubs – Brisbane, Newcastle and Gold Coast, with Manly starting its premiership defence by taking on the Broncos at Lang Park.

If any thing was needed to ram home the fact that this season constituted a brand new ball game, it was the manner in which Brisbane thrashed the premiers 44-10 in the opening match of the season. The grand final party was well and truly over. The Brisbane team was stacked with Queensland State of Origin and Australian Test stars – Rohan Hancock, Allan Langer, Greg Conescu, Gene Miles, Colin Scott, Brian Neibling, and were captained by arguably the most gifted and controversial player in the game at that time, Wally Lewis. Manly were behind 14-6 at half-time and had no answer to Brisbane's second half onslaught.

'Brisbane came into the competition in 1988 and all of a sudden it was like a mini State of Origin match, with the locals well and truly behind their team,' says Cliff. 'Gene Miles, who I rate as the toughest opponent I faced during my career, just hammered us. Just when you thought you had him covered and went in for the tackle, he would use those big legs of his and brush you aside. If you tackled him the wrong way, you'd come off second best.'

The Sea Eagles regrouped after the loss to Brisbane, winning its next three matches by huge margins. After defeating North Sydney 44-18, Manly turned on champagne football in the record 64-12 thrashing of the once-mighty Parramatta team. Cliff bagged a hat-trick of tries on the day and backed up with a non-stop effort in the following match against newcomers Newcastle, setting up four of his team's seven tries.

Manly then faced old sparring partners Balmain on a wet Easter Saturday at Leichhardt Oval. Points were at a premium in the dour match, with Cliff's intercept try in the first half comprising the Sea Eagles only-scoring movement in the 8-6 loss. Lack of consistency proved to the burning question during the ensuing months, defeating Wests, losing 22-0 to Penrith at Brookvale Oval, before a further loss to Souths on Anzac Day. In one of the biggest controversies of the year, Souths was subsequently stripped of its two competition points after illegally playing a 17-year-old President's Cup player, Scott Wilson.

Cliff was rewarded for his good early season form with his selection for City Origin. The previous year, the NSWRL had changed the format of the traditional City-Country clash to make it a strictly 'place of origin' match. Because Cliff played his initial grade football at Cronulla, he was deemed to be a city player despite describing himself as 'a bushie' at heart. Des Hasler was Cliff's halfback partner with selectors choosing Terry Lamb at lock. Cliff played his part in City's 20-18 win over Country and was duly named in NSW's starting line-up for the initial State of Origin match of the year.

1988 marked the opening of the Sydney Football Stadium, a high-tech venue that was quickly being regarded as something of a white elephant. Hammered by bad press over its design (without a roof left it open to the elements) and the cost to attend matches (the league made the fatal mistake of having a set price of $32 for all tickets) a crowd of just over 11,000 watched the City-Country fixtures. The NSWRL hoped for a better response in the State of Origin series, but the situation was not helped by the late withdrawal of Wally Lewis through injury. It was to the first time Lewis had missed a State of Origin match since the inception of the series in 1980.

The first State of Origin match played at the SFS, which drew a disappointing crowd of 26,441, witnessed the arrival of a new star, Allan Langer. Despite the fact that NSW was hosting two of the three matches for the first time in Origin history, Blues fans were slow to get behind their team - and the match wasn't even live on television! With Paul Vautin deputising for the injured 'King' Wally, Queensland rushed to a 26-6 lead after two brilliant tries by Allan Langer set up an early 12-6 advantage. Late tries to Mark McGaw and Andrew Ettingshausen made the final score a respectable 26-18, but the loss was widely unexpected and selectors responded by sacking six players for the return match – Jonathon Docking, Brian Johnston, Noel Cleal, Les Davidson, Royce Simmons and Cliff Lyons.

'It was very frustrating because my form never changed,' remembers Cliff, 'and yet after being good enough to be picked for the first State of Origin match, I was dropped for the second and then recalled for the third. It took the selectors a long time to realise that to win State of Origin matches you had to stick with players who had proven themselves at that level. It's a well-known fact that Queensland did well in those years because they kept the same players, year in and year out, regardless of club form.'

Cliff's sacking could not have come at a worse time. After the Second State of Origin match, the Australian Test team was being selected for the Centennial Anglo-Australian Test match against the Great Britain. Not surprisingly, following a further eight positional changes, the NSW team again failed to gel and was beaten in Brisbane, 16-6. Cliff enjoyed some personal consolation when Manly, minus Test stars Daley, O'Connor and Vautin as well as the injured Dale Shearer, thrashed a second-rate Great Britain side 30-0 at Brookvale Oval. The match also marked the first grade debut of a local teenager named Geoff Toovey.

'Geoff looked like a choir boy when he came into grade,' Cliff remembers. ' He was absolutely fearless in defence, taking on the bigger forwards - and often coming off second best, but he was a champion halfback in the making.' Lyons and Toovey would form a formidable halfback partnership that would last the best part of a decade, and a firm friendship. As unlikely as it seemed, the Manly junior and the journeyman from the bush shared a common element of history. 'After I got to know him better, I found out that Geoff's grandfather served in World War II alongside my grandfather and his brother,' says Cliff. Incredibly, the contribution of Cliff's grandfather and granduncle was not recognised by the Australian government at the time because Aboriginals were deemed not to be Australian citizens. It would be another three decades until the two men's service records were recognised and medals awarded to them.

Cliff's recall for the third State of Origin match followed the withdrawal of regular halves Peter Sterling and Terry Lamb because of injury. The Blues camp was rocked by the sacking of Manly front rower Phil Daley after the Manly prop left camp without permission to visit his pregnant wife. Cliff's former Norths team-mate Steve Hanson, the player with whom Cliff first represented City Seconds in 1985, replaced Daley. With local support dwindling to just 16,000 in the dead rubber, NSW dominated the first 25 minutes to lead 18-6. However, Queensland put on 32 points including seven spectacular tries to completely rout the Blues, 38-22.

Cliff put the disappointment of the State of Origin series behind him to concentrate on bread and butter issues, his great consistency at club level. After losing to Easts 22-18, Manly lost only once in nine matches. The last of these, a spirited 8-4 win over Balmain at Brookvale, marked the return of Kevin Ward. It was also the match in which Balmain was denied a match-winning try after Steve Roach, one of four Tiger players to be sin-binned by referee Greg McCallum, was penalised for punching Phil Daley in an off-the-ball incident.

Disappointingly, Manly sacrificed a top three position in the semi-finals with a shock 23-20 loss to Wests in the penultimate match of the regular season. Manly approached the finals with the knowledge that coach Bob Fulton was standing down after six years at the helm of the club and that reserve grade coach Alan Thompson was his likely successor. Both Manly and Penrith had to win to secure a place in the semi-finals but the realisation that Fulton was ending his stint as coach was enough in itself to motivate the Sea Eagles to coolly account for the Panthers, 18-4, in front of a record Penrith crowd.

This loss relegated Penrith to a midweek play-off for fifth place against Balmain, a spiteful match in which Steve Roach was sent off and subsequently suspended for the remainder of the year after being cited for an incident involving Penrith's Chris Mortimer. Just as Cliff Lyons had done the previous year, Roach attempted to serve the four week suspension handed to him in England and thereby be available if the Tigers made the grand final but the move was subsequently over-ruled by the NSWRL.

Despite the fact that Balmain had only days to back-up after its mid-week win over Penrith, Manly was strangely flat and unconvincing in the minor preliminary semi-final. The Tigers led 13-0 at half-time and, with forwards Noel Cleal, Phil Daley and Kevin Ward replaced uninjured by their clearly disappointed coach, Manly was out-gunned 19-6. While Balmain would go on to win consecutive matches against Canberra and Cronulla before ultimately losing to Canterbury in the grand final, Manly was left to ponder its inability to mount a credible title defence.

During the 1988-89 off-season Cliff rejoined Leeds for another winter of English rugby league. The coach of Leeds was former Great Britain international and former Manly legend, Mal Reilly. 'We had a wonderful time in England on our second trip, the people at Leeds were fantastic,' says Karen. 'Dave Heron, the captain of Leeds, and his wife Yvonne were wonderful to us, as was Garry

Schofield and his wife and of course, Malcolm Reilly. We found lots of friends in England. Sam Backo and Andrew Ettingshausen played at Leeds with Cliff, Kevin Ward and Ronny Gibbs were at Castleford while Paul Vautin and Michael O'Connor were at St Helens.'

This time Cliff and Karen took Cliff's son Shane with them but Karen, seven months pregnant with their first child, was anxious to return home for the birth of their baby. 'I kept cancelling my trip home because I was trying to hedge my bets and stay in England as long as I could. I didn't want to leave Cliff and Shane over there on their own.' In early January 1989, a daughter was born nine weeks premature at Yorkshire Hospital.

The day his daughter was born, Cliff had to board a bus to travel to St Helens and play against his Manly team-mates. 'Cliff couldn't wait to tell 'Fatty' and Mick and although he had been up all night, there was no way he was going to miss the match,' Karen says. 'As he hopped on the bus, he said to his Leeds team-mates, "Well fellas, I've got myself a little Yorkshire lass!" Dave Heron, the club captain, pulled Cliff aside and said in all seriousness, "Gee Cliff, what about Karen?"' The baby girl, eventually named Courtney, spent six weeks in intensive care. The Directors' wives got together and arranged for my mum to travel to England. Mum flew directly from Australia to Manchester and when she arrived at the hospital, the nurses erected a sign, *"Welcome Grandma from Australia from your little Yorkshire Rose"*.

Cliff enjoyed enormous success with Leeds in 1988-89, the club winning the final of the Yorkshire Cup against Castleford. In October, he was selected for the 'Rest of the World,' a team made up of English-based International players, against Great Britain. Captained by his former Norths team-mate Mark Graham and containing Australian players Dale Shearer, Mick O'Connor, Steve Ella, Allan Langer, Sam Backo, Noel Cleal and Gavin Miller, Cliff was chosen as a reserve for the match but took the field in place of

Cleal who took an injury into the match. Great Britain won a tight contest 30-28, the official match report stating, 'While Ella showed fleeting glimpses of his brilliance, it remained a mystery as to how he gained inclusion ahead of magical Cliff Lyons, whose first touch created a try for Peter Brown (NZ).'

Karen and Cliff remain indebted to the people of Leeds for their kindness and hospitality. 'The doctors and nurses were marvellous – nothing was too much trouble for them,' Karen says. While the newest addition to the Lyons' family gathered strength in hospital, Cliff fulfilled his club commitments. 'It was a really stressful time when Courtney was born,' she remembers. 'Cliff got next to no sleep so he asked Malcolm Reilly for a week off from playing. Malcolm suggested that Cliff sit on the bench for the next match and of course, he ended up playing anyway.'

Before returning to Australia, Cliff was asked to go to London to film a NSWRL commercial for the coming season. That promotion turned out to be Tina Turner's *What You Get is What You See*, the predecessor of the highly-successful *Simply the Best* advertisement that took the game into the 1990s. The American soul star was working in London at the time and the advertising agency needed film of Australian rugby league players interacting with Turner. Cliff and Gavin Miller fitted the bill perfectly because they were already in England and both enjoyed the encounter.

After Cliff's arrival back in Australia, in what was one of the happiest years of his personal life following the birth of his daughter, the 1989 rugby league season turned out to be one of the most morale-shattering years in the forty-two-year history of the Manly Club. Hindsight is a wonderful thing but it is a luxury not readily afforded in the professional world of rugby league. A decade later, Cliff says of the tumultuous 1989 season, 'As a coach, Alan Thompson did what he had to do but put simply, the players didn't perform on the football field.'

It is now apparent that Alan Thompson did not stand a chance of emulating the success Bob Fulton enjoyed in his six years as coach of the club. In the late 1980s, huge contracts were being offered to Sydney-based players to go to England and play as many as twenty matches between the end of the Australian season and the start of the next. In the 1988-89 off-season, before Thompson had the chance to stamp his imprimatur on Manly's first grade team, Michael O'Connor, Paul Vautin and Cliff Lyons - players integral to the club's success, were playing in England. O'Connor told Roy Masters in the book *Inside Rugby League*, 'I came back from England a little bit late, with injuries and, apart from not being as fit as normally I would be, I was also mentally stale.'

At the time, over-familiarity with Bob Fulton's coaching methods was blamed for Manly's poor start to the season but moreover, it was a case of the club's leading players being jaded and carrying injuries. Having climbed the premiership mountain in 1987, Manly needed a whole new culture – a new challenge, and the luckless Alan Thompson, having been with the club since his days as a junior, was not the one to give the club a new direction. For the first time since the beginning of the decade, Manly did not make the semi-finals.

Manly started the 1989 season with a 22-20 loss to Parramatta in an exciting match at Parramatta Stadium. The Sea Eagles threw everything at the Eels before narrowly losing but when the losing streak extended to the opening three matches, Manly was already weathering a media storm. The Sea Eagles recorded a much-needed win with a 16-12 victory over Norths, via a questionable try to Cliff Lyons who appeared to be off -side when fielding a bomb, but then won only one more match from their next six encounters.

'It wasn't as if we weren't trying or that Thompson couldn't coach,' recalls Cliff, 'it was just that everything we tried just didn't come off. We had lost our touch and our confidence.' Nothing exemplifies this better than the 9-8 loss to Balmain, a match in which Mick O'Connor scored all his side's points before Balmain hooker Benny Elias landed the winning field goal with three minutes to spare. It was heart-breaking stuff for coach Alan Thomspon, who was forced to concede to the press that the club was indeed 'in trouble'.

Despite the club's perilous position, Paul Vautin and Michael O'Connor were allowed to return to England in May and play for St Helens in the Wembley Cup final. While the pair were away, Manly ground out a hard-fought 14-2 win over Wests, with Noel Cleal as captain and Cliff returning to the centres for the first time in years. In England, O'Connor and Vautin suffered the ignominy of playing in a St Helens team thrashed 27-nil by Wigan. Champion Wigan coach Graham Lowe was about to enter the Manly drama.

The club's poor form created unaccustomed tension within the club, a feeling Cliff had not encountered since his season with Norths in 1985. Midway through the season, Thompson's position as coach was already under pressure and captain Paul Vautin, who showed his loyalty by calling on the club to give the coach a fair go, was struggling to regain his best form. In an effort to spark some pride back in the club following the humiliating 36-10 loss to premiership front-runners Souths, Chief Executive Doug Daley allegedly offered any player who was unhappy at Brookvale a release from their contract before the June 30 deadline. At the time Daley's 'offer' was met with roaring silence and Manly answered the challenge with a hard-fought 22-12 win over Easts. Cliff returned to his best in the 24-10 win over St George in the next match. Down 10-2, Lyons set up a try for Dale Shearer, put in a grubber kick for David Ronson's four-pointer and then capped a great return to form with a 60 metre intercept try.

In June Dale Shearer created headlines when he openly stated that he wanted out of the club. Just when Manly looked to be regaining some form, Shearer informed Daley that he would accept the offer and return to Queensland to play with the Broncos. Incensed, Daley said that the offer had been withdrawn but Shearer started legal action against the club and was eventually released from his obligations. As recently as March, 2000 on Channel 9's Sunday version of the *Footy Show*, Shearer admitted that leaving Manly was the biggest mistake of his career. 'If I had stayed with Manly I would still be playing there,' Shearer said, reflecting on his subsequent moves to Brisbane, Gold Coast, Easts, South Queensland Crushers and North Queensland Cowboys.

Manly defeated defending premiers Canterbury 28-10, after tries to Shearer and Lyons set up an early 12-0 lead. In late June, with Vautin, O'Connor, Shearer and Des Hasler backing up from State of Origin duty, Manly were thrashed by cellar-dwellers Gold Coast, 29-8. Former Manly junior Mike Eden, who achieved his law degree while playing with the Sea-Gulls and later acted as Cliff's manager for a short time, carved-up the Sea Eagles to set up a 20-0 lead after 29 minutes of play. Despite impressive victories over Parramatta (30-8) and Brisbane (the 16-8 win was the club's first against the Broncos), without the club's Test stars who were touring New Zealand, the fates of Thompson and Paul Vautin were already sealed.

Following his return from New Zealand where he was vice-captain in Australia's victorious Test team, word was leaked that the club was reticent to extend premiership-winning captain Paul Vautin's contract. The close-knit Manly community and the Sea Eagles' team were equally upset. In the win against Newcastle at Brookvale Oval, fans voiced their anger, the feeling being that Vautin was being punished for his open support of the coach. Late in the year, when Manly offered Vautin an incentive contract worth barely half his existing contract, pride saw him leave the club to play with Easts.

Manly struggled under a growing toll of injuries to Lyons, Shearer, Vautin, Hasler, Cochrane and Daley and fell to Norths and

Penrith in consecutive weeks. At the conclusion of the year Thompson was told the game's worst kept secret - that his services would not be required for 1990. He was to be replaced by Graham Lowe who was appointed manager-coach. This was the first time since the club's foundation year in 1947 that a coach who had not played with Manly was given the first grade side.

Thompson later lamented that he had never been a part of the club's long-term plan and felt that he was only 'warming the seat' until Lowe had finished his commitments with super club Wigan. Despite Thompson's legendary status with the club (his 263 club games was a record until bettered by Cliff in the late 1990s) the sad fact was that the Sea Eagles finished in twelfth place, the club's worst season on record.

'I feel if Alan Thompson had have been given another year, he would have turned it around,' says Cliff. 'We finished the year with a draw against Balmain, and the Tigers made the grand final that year, and a win against Wests. We had a much better run without injuries the following year. The club bought players of the calibre of Tony Iro, Martin Bella and Ian Roberts and we made the semi-finals.'

At the end of the season the Lyons family retreated from the pressures of a professionally unrewarding year and went to Gundagai for a break. Manly's internal strife and Cliff's own battle with injuries saw any chance of representative football evaporate. On the positive side, Cliff had been the club's equal-leading try-scorer with a modest total of nine tries and had tried to produce his best efforts in what was an inconsistent season for the club.

Little did he know that the next twelve months would provide him with the realisation of his dream of playing for Australia.

CHAPTER SEVEN

Gold 'Dally M'

Graham Lowe came to Manly in 1990 with the express goal of winning a Sydney premiership – the only achievement that he hadn't attained during an extraordinary career. A premiership-winning coach in the North Island town of Otahuhu in the 1970s, Lowe actually wrote the New Zealand Rugby League Coaching Manual. A centre in Lowe's team was Mark Graham, a future Kiwi Test captain and coach of Auckland. When Lowe moved to Queensland to take over as coach of Brisbane Norths in 1979, he lured Mark Graham to Australia, shifting him to the forward pack and winning the Brisbane premiership the following year. During the next two decades, the pair formed a professional association that endured until Lowe was replaced as Chief Executive of the Auckland Warriors in March, 2000.

In 1983 as coach of the New Zealand Test team, Lowe orchestrated a stunning victory over Australia in the Second Test at Lang Park. Previously unbeaten on the 1982 Kangaroo Tour, Australia was completely outplayed by the Kiwis, 19-12. As coach of Wigan in the 1980's, Lowe achieved both Challenge Cup and Championship success. Chief Executive of the ARL, and former

Manly supremo, Ken Arthurson was astutely aware of Lowe's talents as a coach and the following encounter which took place at the end of the Sea Eagles' premiership-winning season certainly turned the club's attention in Lowe's direction.

In his book *Simply the Best*, author Adrian McGregor relates the story of how Lowe and Wigan's Chief Executive Maurice Lindsay approached Ken Arthurson regarding the possibility of reviving the World Club Challenge concept which was conducted briefly in the mid-1970s. So confident were Ken Arthurson and Manly Chief Executive Doug Daley of victory, that the always-diplomatic Arthurson suggested that the $50,000 prize money be shared evenly among the two sides. If Lindsay's response - 'No. Winner take all!' was a surprise, then it was nothing compared to the subsequent manner in which Wigan defeated the Sydney champions, 8-2.

At the end of the 1988-89 English season, Wigan released Lowe from his contract in order to allow him to return to Australia and take on the coaching role at Manly. The English club showed incredible understanding of Lowe's desire to leave, no doubt realising there was no point in keeping a coach who had other things on his mind, but also in gratitude of Lowe for his success with the club. However, their generosity stopped short of allowing star Kiwi import Kevin Iro to break his contract and link with Lowe at Manly. Iro would have to wait another twelve months to join his brother Tony at the Sea Eagles.

'Graham was a very intense character – always on about "stats" and "yardage" and "mistake rates",' remembers Cliff. 'He is also a very likeable person – very charismatic. He lived close-by to us at Dee Why and we got to know him quite well. He was a change of culture for everyone at the club but once we got to know him, the changes worked out to be pretty good.'

Lowe was granted sweeping powers at Manly – first grade coach, team manager and recruitment officer. Rounding of the signing of

Martin Bella from Norths, Ian Roberts from Souths and Kiwi international Tony Iro, Lowe travelled to Auckland in May to secure the services of up-and-coming, Rugby Union fullback Matthew Ridge. The shadow fullback for the All Blacks and a junior Kiwi Rugby Union international, Ridge's mid-season signing turned out to be the coup of the year. Impressively, the club's four new recruits played Test football in 1990 – Ridge, in a World Cup qualifying match for New Zealand against Great Britain just six games after switching codes.

'Graham Lowe was great in the way he pushed for Cliff during the representative season,' says Karen, but still the State selectors failed to take notice. Test coach Bob Fulton had first-hand experience of Cliff's ability to consistently produce the goods under pressure and always knew that he would not let anyone down if given the opportunity. Although Lyons' representative career had lost momentum since he last played for NSW in 1988, the lure of a Kangaroo Tour at the end of the year was very real.

The 1990 season opened in dynamic fashion to the sounds of Tina Turner belting out her newly recorded rugby league anthem, *Simply the Best*. Manly started the season with a return to the club's characteristic dashing style of play, winning the Nissan Sevens tournament at Parramatta Stadium on March 11. Not only was the $60,000 prize money a quick return on the club's investment in its future, Cliff Lyons' try and two goals was a highlight of Manly's 24-22 win over the Eels in the final. If ever a player seemed custom-built for a seven-a-side tournament, it was Lyons. The quixotic master of the cross-field run, Lyons dazzled the crowd of over 25,000 and finished as co-leading point-scorer in the competition with 30 points. His cousin Graham Lyons, a burly winger with Souths, was the leading try-scorer in the tournament with seven tries – his solitary goal tying with Cliff for most points scored by an individual.

Manly started the long journey back to be a major force in the game with a hard-fought 14-12 win over close rivals Balmain in the opening round of the 1990 season. Down 12-0, the Sea Eagles wrested the lead late in the match despite a torrential downpour that resulted in the referee taking the unprecedented step of asking rival captains Ben Elias and Michael O'Connor if they wanted to abandon the game. Des Hasler was selected in the centres following the early-season form of Cliff at five-eighth with Geoff Toovey at halfback. After Manly grafted out an impressive win against Balmain, it followed this with a convincing 28-12 victory over Newcastle.

The club then experienced its teething period under Lowe, losing consecutive matches to Penrith, Brisbane and North Sydney. The 14-12 loss to Brisbane at Lang Park, the match in which Ian Roberts made his debut for the Sea Eagles following his return from injury, was unfortunate in that the match was won by a controversial 'try' incorrectly awarded to Kerrod Walters. Referee Graham Annesley spent the next four months in reserve grade after it was discovered that Walters had lost the ball over the line and the referee was poorly positioned to rule on the decision.

Manly then recorded good wins against Wests and Parramatta but despite Cliff's consistency at five-eighth, he could not win selection in the City teams. With selectors opting for perennial club performer Terry Lamb, Cliff subsequently missed selection in the State of Origin series – a situation that did not augur well for the end of year Kangaroo Tour. Cliff's cousin Graham, a South junior with a deceptive turn of pace, fared better – scoring four tries for City Firsts before playing in all three matches in NSW's series win.

Following back-to-back losses to Canterbury and Canberra at the WACA (an early bid by the NSWRL to gauge interest in rugby league in Perth), Manly put together a seven-match winning sequence that propelled the club into the top three on the premiership table. The Sea Eagles scored 102 points to 8 in the first three of these matches, including consecutive 34-0 thrashings of

Easts and Gold Coast. The match against Easts, at the now long-forgotten venue of Henson Park, brought Cliff back into contact with his former premiership-winning captain Paul Vautin who was doing it tough with the Roosters.

In the 26-20 win over Souths in the next match, Lyons faced two young Rabbitohs who would later play an important part in Manly's ascendancy in the mid 1990s. Terry Hill, a talented Souths junior, scored after just forty seconds of play while Mark Carroll, who like Lyons grew up in Sydney's western suburbs, tore into the Manly pack early in the game. The two players looked to have set a platform for an unlikely Souths victory until Cliff turned a 20-all scoreline into a late victory when he set up the winning try for Craig Hancock.

On the same weekend, legendary five-eighth Wally Lewis broke his arm in Brisbane's narrow 18-14 win over St George. This ruled the incumbent Australian captain out of the Test against France four days later - a match in which the unheralded Mark Carroll was selected as a reserve forward. Although it wasn't apparent at the time, Lewis' injury was to have an indirect impact on Cliff's representative career.

Although gathering momentum in the run-up to the semi-finals, Lowe was dissatisfied with the air of complacency creeping into his team, with a 22-4 win over Illawarra and a last minute, 10-6 defeat of St George. Manly's 24-10 victory over Balmain in the following match was the next installment in the long line of controversial games against the Tigers. In front of a parochial Brookvale Oval crowd, and with five minutes remaining, Steve Roach was marched by referee Eddie Ward after the volatile Balmain forward was reported by a touch judge for a high tackle. Roach made then two cardinal errors - patting the referee on the head before he left and giving the touch judge 'a spray' on his way from the field. Roach was subsequently suspended for four weeks and fined $5,000.

Losses to Newcastle and Penrith confirmed Lowe's fears that the Sea Eagles were taking success for granted but in the last month before the semi-finals, wins over Brisbane, Norths and Wests (with seven top Manly players missing) - capped by the 30-4 thumping of Parramatta – helped secure fourth place in the play-offs. Cliff scored two tries against the Eels and carried this good form into the sudden-death semi-final against big-match rivals Balmain.

After Balmain defeated Newcastle in a midweek play-off, the minor preliminary semi-final became the last avenue for retiring Balmain captain Wayne Pearce to win a premiership before the end of his playing career. In a comprehensive shutout, Lyons orchestrated the 16-0 win over the Tigers to give the likeable Pearce a send-off that unfortunately wasn't in the script. Cliff crossed for the opening try of the match, put in the kick that led to Geoff Toovey scoring and then played an important role in the lead-up work to Tony Iro's try.

Manly took on Brisbane in the minor semi-final in their next match, the Broncos reeling from the thrashing handed out by Penrith on Father's Day the previous week. Manly was clear favourites for the match but the Broncos showed an early glimpse of the class that would win the premiership in two years time. Brisbane led 6-2 at half-time with the scores delicately balanced at 6-4 with 25 minutes remaining. Ian Roberts was in menacing form until a hamstring injury ended his season and any thoughts of Kangaroo selection. In the 71st minute, Ridge missed a difficult penalty attempt that would have tied the match before replacement back Peter Jackson scored the winning try to give Brisbane a 12-4 win.

Despite the disappointment of faltering when so close to the grand final, Graham Lowe had returned the Sea Eagles to the semi-final arena within twelve months of taking up his appointment. Three days later, on September 11, 1990, the rugby league *glitterati* turned out in formal attire for the 'Dally M' Awards at the Sydney

Entertainment Centre. Cliff, who was leading the polling when the awards went behind closed doors in the final month of the season, knew that his form had been consistent in the weeks leading up to the semi-finals. An early indication into how the judges voted was given when Cliff nosed arch-rival Terry Lamb out of the 'Five-Eighth of the Year' Award. Lamb had dominated the positional award since winning his 'Gold Dally M' in 1984, and Cliff was hopeful that this early success would be an early indication for the 'big one'.

At the Entertainment Centre, the Manly players sat together several rows from the front. 'Doug Daley (Manly Chief Executive) had it all arranged,' Karen Lyons remembers. 'Doug must have known something, because he was sitting just behind Cliff so he was one of the first to congratulate him. When the first runner-up was announced, (Norths half) Jason Martin leaned across and gave Cliff a nod, as if to say "It's yours mate, you've won it".' Cliff edged out rival halves Ricky Stuart and Jason Martin to win the gold statuette. It was to be *his* night.

One week after winning the Gold 'Dally M' for Player of the Year', fate would play its hand in Cliff's favour. On September 18, Wally Lewis was controversially ruled out of the Kangaroo Tour when he failed a fitness test on his injured arm. ARL Medical Officer, Dr Nathan Gibbs ruled that Lewis' radius bone in his left arm had not fully recovered from the break and had only mended on the surface of the bone. The news that Wally Lewis would not be touring with the Kangaroos undoubtedly helped Lyons' selection as did team-mate Michael O'Connor's unreported act of unselfishness.

'Some time before the Kangaroo squad was even selected, Michael O'Connor rang Cliff and informed him that he was going to pull out of the tour because he was injured,' remembers Karen. 'He told us that by announcing that he was pulling out early, he hoped this would open up the door a little wider for Cliff. It was a nice gesture but we were all hoping Cliff would be selected anyway.'

Cliff's career had matured like fine wine, his consistency during the season winning a P&O Cruise from the club's sponsor as Player of the Year. However, because of the growing demands of their young family, it would be another two years before he and Karen could actually enjoy it. Having just been named the best player in the premiership, was it too much to hope for a belated selection for Australia? He certainly deserved it, but sometimes even that is not enough. Complicating matters was the fact that Karen was expecting their second child in December.

'Before the squad was announced,' Karen says, 'Bob Fulton rang us at home and I answered the phone. He asked, "Is it alright if I take your husband away for a couple of months?" I said that I would love him to.' On the night Canberra defeated Penrith in the grand final, Cliff waited for the 28-man squad to be read out on radio just in case he hadn't heard what Bob Fulton had told him. Alexander, Belcher, Bella, Carroll, Cartwright, Daley, Elias, Ettingshausen, Fittler, Geyer, Gillespie, Hancock, Hasler, Johns, Langer, Lazarus, Lindner, *Lyons* .... 'Rocky' had finally made it.

Cliff's brother Colin adds, 'I've always had an uncanny knack of knowing Cliff's future – even better than knowing my own. Playing for Australia was one of those things in my mind that was just going to happen for Cliff. I knew it from his earliest days playing for Gundagai. We all did.' Cliff joined teammates Des Hasler and Martin Bella in the squad, a little gloss taken off Manly's fine achievement by the unavailability of Michael O'Connor and Ian Roberts because of injury.

There is a lovely photo of a proud Cliff Lyons standing in the front yard of his Queenscliff home, decked out in his Australian Kangaroo Tour blazer and holding infant daughter Courtney. The photo was taken by an equally proud Karen Lyons, who despite being seven months pregnant with the couple's second child, was happy to see her husband fulfill his ambition. Lyons had played an

Two crocks on the mend – Michael O'Connor and Cliff Lyons, 1991.

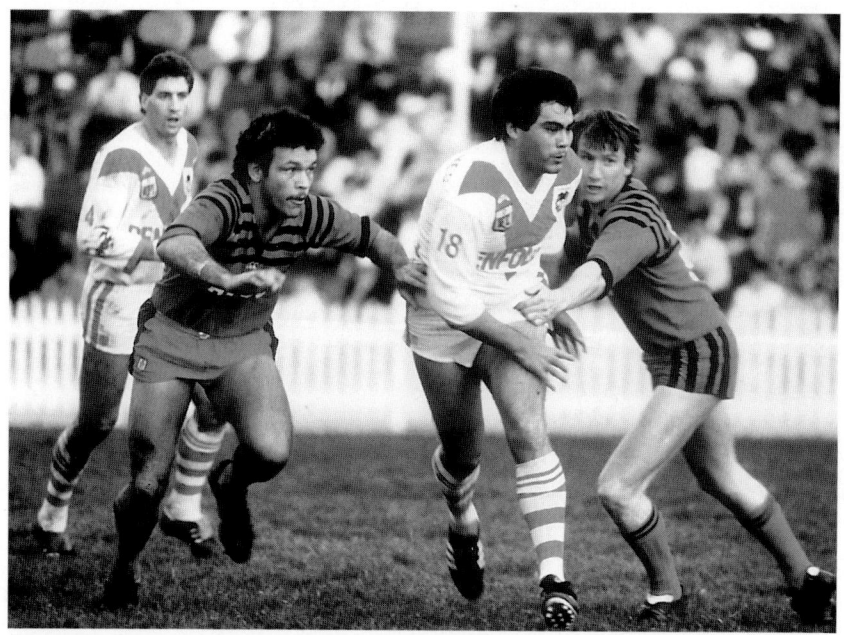

Chasing success at Norths, 1985... team-mate Andrew Simons is also pictured.

NSW celebrate their win in the fourth State of Origin match in Los Angeles, 1987 ... (from left to right) Brian Johnston (sitting), Jonathon Docking, Noel Cleal, Peter Sterling, Mark McGaw (sitting), Peter Tunks, Les Davidson and Cliff Lyons.

At Manly, 1986.

Cliff and Phil Daley walk from the field after a victory against the Eels at Parramatta Stadium, 1987. The little boy at the left of the picture is Cliff's eldest son, Shane.

1987 Grand Final tryscoring sequence 1 –
Cliff ducks under the tackle of Steve Walters and Chris O'Sullivan...

1987 Grand Final tryscoring sequence 2 –
... surges for the try line...

1987 Grand Final tryscoring sequence 3 –
... and scores the opening try of the 1987 grand final against Canberra.

Visiting Disneyland after the Fourth State of Origin match in Los Angeles,
1987. Peter Sterling and Peter Tunks are pictured with Cliff.

Manly celebrate their 1987 grand final win. Cliff holds the Giltinan Shield with Phil Daley.

Cliff and youngest daughter Gabrielle.

Ron Gibbs and Cliff Lyons celebrate Manly's 1987 grand final win.
Cliff's son Shane is beside him.

integral role in Manly's success in the Nissan Sevens, appeared in all 22 matches and in two semi-finals, finished equal top try-scorer for the club, was named 'Gold Dally M' Player of the Year and, capping a remarkable season, was chosen for the Kangaroo Tour of England and France. Only Ashes glory waited.

Those of us among the thousands of Australian Rugby League fans who sat bleary-eyed in the early hours of November 11, 1990 and watched Mal Meninga score the winning try in the Second Test, may recall that it was Cliff Lyons who cleverly switched play and gave Ricky Stuart the ball – the start of the Canberra halfback's 90 metre run to the try-line. Some may even remember the equally brilliant try Cliff scored just after half-time. Ken Arthurson, the then Executive Chairman of the ARL, was sitting ashen-faced with the rest of the Australian contingent on that cold Manchester evening contemplating a Second Test defeat and the loss of the Ashes.

'The try that Meninga scored would never have been possible except for the fact that Cliff got away a great pass to Ricky Stuart – in a situation when nobody thought a pass could have been given,' says Arthurson. 'Cliff played superbly in the deciding two Tests in England. Bob Fulton has said, and I've said it publicly on a number of occasions, had Cliff Lyons not been selected in the Second Test, Australia would not have retained the Ashes.'

CHAPTER EIGHT

On Tour with the Kangaroos

When the Kangaroos landed in Manchester in October 1990 the 28 players and sundry officials decked out in gaudy green and gold tracksuits topped off with a Greg Norman hat were whisked away by a tour coach emblazoned with a huge *Kangaroos '90'* sign. The 'Aussie tourist' look was completed by the addition of 100 two-dozen packs of Fourex beer supplied by major sponsors Castlemaine. When pressed by an English media still reeling after the withdrawal of international showcard Wally Lewis, coach Bob Fulton stressed the superiority of this squad compared to the undefeated 1982 and 1986 Tours. He stated to the press that he had 28 players at his disposal and every one of them could play at Test level - and promptly supported this view by using 25 players in the five Tests played on tour.

It is a reality of all Kangaroo Tours that the players divide into two groups – the Kangaroos (the established Test players) and the Emus (the remainder). Cliff started the tour happily enough as an *emu,* making his debut in the green and gold in the second match of the tour. Lyons kept to the card-playing contingent of the team, forming a firm friendship with Ricky Stuart and spending the many long hours on the tour bus and in the hotel playing euchre and poker with Stuart, Ben Elias and Allan Langer.

Tour management's decision to bunk Lyons with aggressive Brisbane winger Mick Hancock was certainly a strange one - Cliff, quietly spoken; Hancock, outwardly abrasive. Hancock, who Cliff can not recall being seen without a mobile phone stuck to his ear, had the dangerous habit early in his career of resisting the tackler and lashing out with his feet. '"Angry" Mick" we called him,' says Cliff. 'He tried to make out that he was as angry off the field as he was on the field but I don't think he was. Mick's a nice bloke.'

St Helens was given the honour of hosting the first match of the tour because it was celebrating its centenary as a club but realistically, the Saints were not considered among the top five teams in England. But as was tradition on Kangaroo Tours, the opening match was a dress rehearsal for the intended Test line-up with Laurie Daley and Allan Langer chosen as the halfback combination. Australia started its Ashes defence by handing St Helens a 34-4 thumping; the only worrying sign for the tourists being the inability of Mal Meninga to land more than one goal from his six attempts. Meninga had played for St Helens in 1989-90 and was something of a sporting icon in the north of England but it was clear that the Ashes contests weren't going to be decided by his goal-kicking.

Coach Bob Fulton continued to experiment with the halfback combination during the tour, exploring every possible combination except the obvious club partnerships – Hasler and Lyons (Manly), Walters and Langer (Brisbane) and Daley and Stuart (Canberra). Lyons joined five other players in making their international debut in the second match of the tour against Wakefield Trinity - Mark Sargent, Kevin Walters, Chris Johns, 19 year-old Brad Fittler, and Cliff's halfback partner Ricky Stuart.

Cliff was the only debutante not to score a try in 36-18 win but Fulton was seething in his assessment of English referee Kevin Allott after Australia finished on the wrong end of a 26-7 penalty count. Allott sent three Australian players from the field as well as sin-binning Des Hasler and Dale Shearer. Mark Carroll was dismissed for fighting, Stuart was sent off on a high tackle charge with a minute remaining, and David Gillespie was marched after the final bell when he was wrongly accused of back-chatting. Allott clearly lost control late in the game and in the aftermath to the controversy, Stuart was exonerated and no penalty was handed down to either Carroll or Gillespie.

In the third match of the tour, against the John Monie-coached Wigan, Fulton again opted for the Daley-Langer combination at halfback with good results. The English Challenge Cup winners had rolled the New Zealand national team earlier in the year but despite vocal support from 25,000 fans, Wigan had no answer to a Test-strength Australian team. Andrew Ettingshausen bagged a hat-trick of tries in the 34-6 win which was a record margin against the reigning club champions and an ominous sign for the Great Britain national team.

The match against Leeds at Headingly provided the Australians with the toughest match of the tour and a vital lead-in to the First Test to be played at Wembley the following week. Cliff, who played in the centres in the previous match against Cumbria and was not required against Leeds, almost missed the team bus back to London because he was catching up with all of his old team-mates. Fired by a clever kicking game from Great Britain Test pivot Garry Schofield, Leeds led 10-2 before the Australian juggernaut got into full speed. The Kangaroos won 22-10 but were rocked by the subsequent news that Mark Carroll had injured his knee and five-eighth Laurie Daley had broken his hand.

The worst was realised when the Kangaroos arrived in London

for the First Test and team medico Dr Nathan Gibbs was able to secret Daley and Carroll away from the media for X-rays. Daley continued to train with the nominated Test squad under the smokescreen of a dislocated finger but on the Wednesday before the match, officially pulled out of the team. This led to the pairing of rival club halves Ricky Stuart and Allan Langer, an untried partnership in the lead-up games on tour. Coupled with the fact that the Australian camp had resettled in South Kensington and was plagued by construction noise at night and traffic jams on the way to training, it was a less than trouble-free preparation for the First Test.

On October 27 an English test record crowd of 52,274 turned out to witness one of the most amazing upsets in Anglo-Australian Test history. Captained by the enigmatic Ellery Hanley, Great Britain stunned Australia, winning 19-12 after the scores were locked at 2-all at half-time. There were seventeen first-half penalty stoppages from French referee Alain Sablayrolles but in fairness, the Lions were the better team in the second half. Hanley set up the first try of the match three minutes into the second half after evading Paul Sironen, stepping out of the tackle of Mark McGaw and chipping over the head of Gary Belcher. Hanley regathered the ball close to the line but after being tackled, dummy half Darryll Powell sent Paul Eastwood over in the corner.

Mal Meninga replied with a try after a good break from Bob Lindner but Hanley responded brilliantly, putting up the kick that led to winger Martin Offiah's try. In contesting the ball before offloading to try-scorer Martin Offiah, Hanley 'hipped' the ever-reliable Gary Belcher before the Australian fullback could grasp the ball. When Garry Schofield landed a field-goal soon after, England led 13-6. Australia was constantly penalised for off-side play, the French referee's interpretation a continuing frustration to the pacy Australian backline. A magnificent individual try by Mark McGaw could have been the signal for a miraculous Australian victory but Garry Schofield, the player who had caused Australia so much trouble at Leeds, produced the clincher when his chip kick resulted in Eastwood's second try. Great Britain missed the conversion but sealed its 19-12 win with a penalty goal two minutes before full-time.

'After the First Test loss I told all the players that I was looking to change the line-up,' Fulton says. 'I copped a lot of stick in the press about it and although we certainly had some good halfbacks on the tour, ultimately I went for Cliffy because I knew how he'd perform under pressure.' Fulton got a look at the Hasler and Fittler partnership in the 26-6 win over Warrington in the next match but when Australia took on Castleford at Weldon Road, Stuart and Lyons were paired for the first time. In other calculated changes in the 28-8 win over Castleford, Fulton chose Elias at hooker, Brad Mackay at lock and Glenn Lazarus in the front row. When Mark McGaw suffered a knee injury and was ruled out of the remainder of the tour, it paved the way for Daley to make his return in the centres.

Ten days before the vital Second Test, Fulton read out the team – Belcher, Ettingshausen, Meninga (c), Daley (replacing McGaw), Hancock, *Lyons*, Stuart (from five-eighth to halfback, replacing Langer), Mackay (for second rower Cartwright), Lindner (shifting from lock to second row), Sironen, Roach, Elias (for Walters) and Lazarus (replacing Bella). 'Cliff rang me at home once he got back to his room,' recalls Karen. 'He couldn't hold his emotion back. "I'm in! I'm in!" he said. Cliff desperately wanted me to catch the next flight over but my doctor said definitely no.'

Allan Langer was given the captaincy duties for the match against Halifax, a sweetener from the selectors after being dropped from the Test side. Australia won easily at Thrum Hall, leading 32-6 at halftime before a Halifax fightback, on the strength of ten second-half penalties, allowed the home team to reduce the full-time deficit to 36-18. When room-mate Michael Hancock was ruled out of the Second Test team because of an ankle injury suffered in the match against Halifax, Cliff realised how quickly fortunes could change on tour. Hancock was replaced in the Test by Cliff's former Manly team-mate 'Rowdy' Shearer.

With Karen unable to travel to England to witness Cliff's Test debut, the Lyons turned their attention to Cliff's mother, Melva. 'When Cliff was selected in the Kangaroo team I was determined to go and see him play,' says Melva. 'I had won $600 but it wasn't enough. Then Karen rang my next door neighbour (we didn't have the phone on then) and I went in to answer it. "Cliff's been selected for the Second Test," she said and I got all excited. "He wants you to come over for the match," and then I burst into tears. There was no way that I could afford it.'

'"No," Karen explained, "we're paying for you to go over." So I ran back to my house to get my diary so I could write down all the details. I was crying and carrying on so much that my neighbour Mrs Sutton and my sister Barbara, who was following me around, thought someone had died. I went in to work and immediately put in for my holidays but I was so excited that I couldn't stop crying so they sent me home.'

Melva Kennedy flew out on the Friday and arrived at Manchester on the Saturday morning of the Test match. She arranged to meet a work friend who was travelling through England at the time and was living at Chester. 'She was two hours late picking me up from Manchester Airport,' Melva recalls. 'Chris Hasler, Des' wife, met me at the airport and looked after me until I was picked up. We had just enough time to shower and make it to the ground. The whole thing was like a dream. I don't know if I was jet-lagged or just over-excited but I couldn't remember anything of the game other that Australia won. Luckily the kids taped the game and I was able to enjoy it when I got back home.'

The only stipulation Cliff placed on his mother was that Melva not 'bother' him in the lead-up to the match. In reality, Cliff had the weight of the world on his shoulders and felt every bit of it. 'For years, I had heard the media say that I couldn't play or that I wasn't a big-game player or that I was easily niggled – any old excuse. Now if we lost, it would be my fault – that "Bozo" picked me because he used to be my Manly coach and not because I deserved it. Here I was 29 years of age and still having to prove myself.' Combined with this was the added worry that Karen could have their baby while he was on the other side of the world.

In a tribute to Cliff's reputation as a play-maker in England, Malcolm Reilly, Cliff's former coach at Leeds in 1988-89, told the *Telegraph Mirror's* Ray Chesterton that Cliff's inclusion more than doubled Australia's attacking potential. 'Lyons will bring much greater creativity to the Australian attack and make outside men like Mal Meninga and Laurie Daley even more dangerous,' Reilly was quoted as saying.

Sensing history was about to be made and the Ashes were to be returned to England for the first time in twenty years 46,000 fans packed Old Trafford for the Second Test. Australia withstood the opening 20 minutes of attack, with Garry Schofield resorting to two early field goal shots in order to break the deadlock. Lyons, Stuart and Daley, the latter player's immaculate passing skills not the least bit betrayed by his broken hand, combined to send Dale Shearer over in the corner before Great Britain was awarded a shot at goal just before the break. Australia led 4-2 at half-time but shortly after the resumption of play, Schofield sent Paul Dixon crashing over for a try to send the Lions to the front, 6-4.

Australia responded with one of the best tries seen in an Ashes Test. No fewer than fifteen sets of hands were involved in a frenetic passing rush that resulted in a miraculous try to Cliff Lyons. Ben Elias handled twice and Cliff touched the ball for the third time as he grounded Andrew Ettingshausen's infield kick. Euphoric after the classic try-scoring moment, Cliff was surprised that the Lions gave him so much space to move. 'Great Britain kept Garry Schofield out of the front line of defence to play a sweeper role,' says Cliff. '"ET" said to me after the match that he saw me on his inside, out of the corner of his eye and just went for it.' We had an understanding of each other's play from our time together at Leeds. Put that try down to our "Leeds connection"'.

Just when Australia seemed to be gaining the ascendancy, but with 12 minutes left on the clock, Ricky Stuart threw a long pass that was intercepted by Paul O'Loughlin. The Great Britain replacement winger was chased all the way to the try-line by Laurie Daley which was enough to spook O'Loughlin from running around underneath the posts. The Australian side, their supporters in the stand and those glued to their television sets back home, breathed a collective sigh of relief when Paul Eastwood, the two-try hero from the First Test, missed the relatively easy conversion.

In a vain attempt to break the 10-all deadlock, Stuart and Elias got in each other's way and both missed with late field-goal attempts. Realistically, as holders of the Ashes trophy, a draw in the circumstances would have been enough to keep the series alive for Australia. When Garry Schofield found the touch-line five metres out from the Australian try-line inside the final five minutes, a draw looked inevitable. That scenario though, did not sit well with the Kangaroos' sense of occasion.

Taking the ball in his hands, Cliff Lyons ran to the left and then quickly doubled back to the right. Shooting a quick pass to Stuart, the Australian halfback took off like a startled rabbit. Inside the Great Britain 20m line, Stuart was coming to the end of his run with cover closing in when he saw the immense shadow of Mal Meninga looming in support. The Australian captain shouldered his way into the clear, bumping opposing centre Carl Gibson out of the way in the process, and took the final pass to dive over. Unbelievably, Australia had lifted to win the match, 14-10.

After two weeks of being under siege from continuous media scrutiny and the spectre of being the first squad since 1956-57 to *lose* the Ashes in England, the pressure had been removed. Cliff made a beeline for his mother. 'We made a poster which said, *"Go Rocky!"*' Melva recalls. 'When the team came out onto the field for their warm-up, you could see Cliff standing with his hands on his hips looking up into the crowd trying to see us. When he finally did, he could clearly see the sign and gave us a big wave.'

There were just two matches scheduled before the deciding Third Test and Australia was not going to be distracted from their steely resolve to retain the Ashes. Hull, whose coach Brian Smith turned over his team to incoming coach Noel Cleal for the night, was easily disposed of before Widnes, captained by Cliff's 'double'- Kiwi forward Kurt Sorensen, became Australia's next victim in the final club game of the tour. The Kangaroos prevailed but there were accusations of eye gouging labelled against their hosts after an acrimonious, 15-8 win.

Fulton retained his successful combination for the deciding Third Test with the atmosphere in the Australian camp in the lead-up to the game decidedly more relaxed. In the week before the match, Ricky Stuart and Laurie Daley even took Cliff's mum with them to a Charlie Pride concert. A capacity crowd of 35,000 packed Elland Road Stadium at Leeds but realistically, Great Britain was never in the match. 'We were a lot surer of ourselves and more comfortable with each other in the Third Test,' says Cliff. 'It was a complete shutout - in our minds they were never going to win.'

Australia led 4-0 at the break after Andrew Ettingshausen scored from a torpedo pass fired by Ricky Stuart, taking advantage of the gap left by injured Great Britain centre Carl Gibson. The try that secured the Ashes came thirteen minutes into the second half after a quiet piece of genius from Cliff. Despite being told by coach Mal Reilly, assistant coach Phil Larder and his Leeds coach David Ward not to rush up in defence when Australian was attacking, Schofield could not resist the temptation of trying to intercept the pass from Stuart to Lyons.

Cliff had seen players try this on him a thousand times – and in matches from Gundagai to Lang Park opposing pivots had often made the mistake of rushing up on him. He also knew that it was a trait of Schofield's game from their time as team-mates at Leeds. Lyons' reply was to accentuate the gap left by the flailing Garry Schofield by stepping off his right foot and darting into the gap. With Meninga in support, Cliff executed a clever, over-the-shoulder pass to his inside, with the Kangaroo captain strolling over under the posts. Australia protected its 10-0 lead in a twenty-minute defensive display that broke the spirits of their opponents. They willed themselves not to concede a try and eight minutes from full-time Elias crossed for the final four-pointer of the match.

Australia had retained the Ashes, 2 Tests to 1. Not *The Invincibles* of '82 or *The Unbeatables* of '86, more like *The Undeniables*!

Back home in Australia, Karen Lyons was joined by Cliff's father Pat and brother Ricky to watch the match. After celebrating Australia's victory and saying good night to her guests, Karen remarked to her mother, who was staying with her in Cliff's absence, that she was going to drive herself to the hospital. Later that morning, after hurriedly seconding Cliff's Manly team-mate Chris White and his wife to mind Courtney, Karen's mother Connie was called to the hospital in time to witness the birth of a baby boy six weeks earlier than expected.

'After the match, we went back to the Ramada and we were invited to a reception thrown by the family of Ben Elias,' says Melva. 'We decided to go back to our hotel and freshen up and when we arrived Cliff was nowhere to be seen. He was gone for about an hour and someone said that he was on the phone to Karen in Sydney.'

Unbeknown to Melva, Cliff was talking to Karen in hospital. Mathew Lyons was born on November 25, 1990 – the day his father played a pivotal role in Australia's retention of the Ashes. 'We thought of naming him "Ashley" because Australia had won the Ashes,' says Melva proudly, 'but I'm glad they settled on Mathew, and so is Matty.'

After the heroics in England, the tour of France was something of an anti-climax. Australia breezed through its four matches on the continent, the only thing that kept Cliff's thoughts from wandering back to home and his new son, was his selection in the two Tests against the French. After thrashing a French President's XIII, 46-18, and a France B line-up 78-6, Australia won the First Test at Avignon 60-4 and the Second Test at Perpignon by a modest 34-10.

'The boys stopped off at Singapore on the way home but I flew straight on through,' says Cliff. 'Looking back, it was something that I had dreamed of doing my whole life and it certainly didn't disappoint. But I couldn't wait to get home. I talked our French interpreter into giving up her seat and arrived home without anyone knowing.'

'Cliff is always one for surprises,' laughs Karen Lyons. 'When he was named "2GB Player of the Year" in 1987, he deliberately didn't tell me that he was being awarded a new car before the grand final so he could see the expression on my face. The same thing happened when the ARL awarded him the Services to Rugby League trophy before the 1995 grand final. When Mathew was born, the media rang and asked if they could come over to the hospital and take a photo of us together. Against my better judgment, I said yes - but only if they sent a copy over to Cliff in England, which they did. Later, they rang back asking if I was going to the airport with the baby to meet Cliff when the Kangaroos returned home. I was really worried that I would be too emotional and everyone would see me lose it.'

Cliff saved all that worry, Karen remembers. 'I arrived home from shopping one morning and Courtney, who had stayed home with Mathew and my parents, was hiding from me in one of the rooms. She came out with an excited look on her face with her father right behind her. Cliff was already home.'

CHAPTER NINE

Papua-New Guinea

On February 7, 1991, Manly coach Graham Lowe underwent emergency surgery at Royal North Shore Hospital to stop the bleeding after suffering a brain haemorrhage. While it was originally thought that he would not be able to continue with the Sea Eagles nor fulfill his commitments as newly appointed coach of Queensland State of Origin, Lowe was quick to get back into training and actually saw the time he spent with his players as therapeutic.

'It was a very serious illness,' Lowe told author Bret Harris in his book *State of Origin: 1980-91*. 'I was advised to take six months off everything. I understood the advice, but I thought the feeling I got from the players would help my rehabilitation. I went to see the Manly players the day after I came out of hospital.' Despite having a potentially fatal blood-clot illness, Lowe not only fulfilled his obligations with Manly – taking the Sea Eagles to the semi-finals, but also guided Queensland to a memorable State of Origin series victory.

The heavy playing schedule of the previous year finally caught up with Cliff in a pre-season match in Auckland. Cliff suffered a damaged medial ligament in his right knee but the injury was relatively minor and he was sidelined for only six weeks. Minus Lyons and Michael O'Connor, who was nursing a broken arm, Manly started the season with a 12-2 loss to Brisbane. The new 'interchange' rule being used turned the Lang Park sideline into a waiting room for players queuing up to get onto the field. While the rule was to require some fine-tuning before becoming an integral part of the game in the 1990s, it was to have a far-reaching affect on many players' careers – not least being that of Cliff Lyons.

'The interchange rule lengthened my career, no doubt about it,' says Cliff of the controversial rule change that changed the face of rugby league. 'It was much more help to the forwards than me. I was a ball-player, an organiser. Although I could see the value in starting the game with a defensive line-up, there was no substitute to actually starting a match, which is the way I would have preferred.' In 1991, Lyons came off the bench twice. By 1993, his matches from the interchange bench had grown to 8. By 1997, when the rule was unlimited interchange, Cliff played in 15 matches from the bench.

At a club function to farewell Cliff in 1999, champion long-distance runner Shelley Taylor Smith gave an inspiring speech about Cliff's longevity and ability to 'go the distance'. 'In many ways Cliff is like a long-distance runner, he gets better in a match when allowed to build-up momentum,' says wife Karen. 'That's why he found it so hard to be benched during the latter part of his career.'

Cliff made his season debut from the interchange bench in the fourth round win against Norths at Brookvale Oval. Manly then won seven consecutive matches, giving the club a share of the lead in the competition. A highlight of the period was the 46-12 thrashing of defending premiers Canberra at Bruce Stadium, Cliff's first full first grade game after coming back from knee surgery. Cliff showed the class that had won him a Test berth the previous year, piloting Manly to an incredible 38-0 lead at half time. It was a game of sheer brilliance from the champion Sea Eagle triumvirate of lock Des Hasler, halfback Geoff Toovey and Lyons. Michael O'Connor scored two tries in a return to his best form while Matthew Ridge landed nine goals.

On Anzac Day, Cliff took his place as five-eighth in the City Origin team alongside team-mates Hasler and Toovey. To cap a tremendous club achievement, the City team was led by Manly captain Michael O'Connor with Ian Roberts in the forward pack. Despite further changes to the eligibility rules which allowed players who started their careers with clubs outside of Sydney to qualify for Country, City still dominated the match, 22-12. Lyons combined excellently with Toovey, setting up a great try for Andrew Ettingshausen to establish an unassailable 16-2 lead.

Lyons was duly selected for State of Origin duty, selectors opting for the Ashes-winning halfback partnership of Cliff and Ricky Stuart. NSW was coached by Canberra mentor Tim Sheens, the premiership-winning coach preferring to rely on the services of Raider team-mates Laurie Daley and Ricky Stuart behind the scrumbase while the squad was in training. This did little for Cliff's confidence and the veteran pivot found himself on the outer before a ball was even kicked. In one of the closest series on record, there were just two points separating the teams in each of the three matches played. Queensland won the opening match 6-4 before NSW captured one of the most memorable and controversial games ever played in State of Origin football.

Just before half time in the second match, Queensland legend Wally Lewis took on fiery young Penrith forward Mark Geyer and the game looked set to erupt. When Geyer was sin-binned for using an elbow to the head of Maroon fullback Paul Hauff, the match was a powder keg ready to ignite despite. The Blues eventually won 14-12 in atrocious conditions at the SFS, via a late try to Mark McGaw and a magnificent conversion by Michael O'Connor from a wide angle and in blinding rain.

Cliff suffered the ignominy of being the only player dropped from NSW's winning State of Origin team for the decider in Brisbane. Tim Sheens had shown his hand when he replaced Lyons late in the second half of the Sydney match with selectors finally bowing to Sheens' wishes and moving centre Laurie Daley to pivot. Considering the second game was played in torrential rain and the conditions did not entirely suit Cliff's free-running style, NSW had still won and Lyons can be excused for feeling hard done by. At the time, Sheens went on record as saying that Cliff's style of play was less effective against teams who directed their large pack of forwards to run at him.

'The whole family were at the after-match function when NSW won the second match and we knew something was on the cards,' recalls Karen Lyons. 'Tim didn't come over and talk to us during the night, nor could he look Clifford in the eye.' Sheens may have felt uncomfortable about contemplating a change of pivot considering the Blues had won the match. It is ironic that when Cliff was offered a *Super League* contract in 1995, had he accepted it was more than likely that he would have linked with Sheens at the North Queensland Cowboys. And there was no denying that Sheens was a fan of Lyons' – the veteran coach was generous in his praise of Cliff's career when Lyons 'first' said goodbye to Brookvale Oval fans following the match against the Cowboys in 1998.

What hurt though was that Cliff was now out of contention for a Test jersey against the visiting New Zealand team – even as a reserve, and his family would not see him play a Test in Australia. Today, Cliff is philosophical about his sacking. 'I certainly wasn't the first five-eighth to be dropped for NSW – they must have used a dozen different players against Wally Lewis during his State of Origin career (the official number is nine between 1980 and 1991). I gave up long ago worrying about what selectors do.' When Daley withdrew before the match, he was replaced by Brad Fittler. Cliff was out of the team.

History shows that Queensland won the third match of the 1991 series 14-12 with Mick O'Connor missing with all four shots at goal after being heavily concussed in a high tackle by Mal Meninga. The win by the Maroons was a fitting finale to the career of retiring Queensland captain Wally Lewis but for Cliff, the real hero of the day was his Manly coach Graham Lowe who had overcome another bout of blood-clotting in his troublesome right leg to climb out of his hospital bed and rejoin the Maroons camp the day before the match. After losing the series decider, Tim Sheens was unceremoniously dumped as coach by the NSWRL when officials were embarrassed by his decision to take the Blues players off the field without waiting for the official presentations.

The Sea Eagles suffered a lapse of form in the middle of the competition, recording one win and a draw from six matches. Why the slump again focused unwarranted media attention on Lowe's health, the reality was that the hectic representative season (three State of Origin matches and three Tests against New Zealand) combined with injuries to star players (Roberts, Hasler, Lyons, O'Connor, Williams and Tony Iro), had hindered the club's premiership quest.

In the run up to the semi-finals, Manly was able to regroup with a series of good wins, especially against semi-final aspirants Canterbury (22-12), Brisbane (26-0) and Norths (15-0) which helped the club to secure third position in the final five. Cliff was in sensational form against the Broncos and had a leading hand in each of his team's four tries. The champion five-eighth's links to his outside backs and his ability to time his passes to perfection dispelled the belief of his State of Origin coach that Cliff was less effective against teams with bigger packs.

Manly's only losses in the two months leading up to the play-offs were one-point losses to eventual semi-finalists Wests and Canberra. The Sea Eagles took on traditional rivals Norths in the major preliminary semi-final. Norths had not won a semi-final since 1952 and despite the resurgence in the club's fortunes, the Bears weren't expected to trouble Manly. Martin Bella who, like Cliff, had come to Manly from Norths, gave his former club some added ammunition when he labelled the Bears 'ordinary' in the week leading up to the match. Norths proved they were anything but ordinary, converting a 16-all scoreline with seven minutes remaining into a stunning 28-16 win.

The sudden-death semi-final against a Canberra team desperately searching for its third consecutive premiership title exemplifies an aspect of Cliff's game not often utilised by his coaches – his captaincy. Lyons was fortunate throughout his career to have played under several captains who had undeniable championship qualities – Paul Vautin, Michael O'Connor, Mal Meninga and Geoff Toovey to name but a few, but he also brought something special to that role – his own quiet resolve to win and an ability to inspire by sheer presence.

Without the services of the injured Ian Roberts, Des Hasler and Michael O'Connor, Graham Lowe named Cliff as captain for the semi-final against the Raiders and shifted him to halfback. Manly's woes were compounded by two factors – the reserve grade team had not won a single match under coach Max Krilich so the depth in the club was questionable, and further injuries to Geoff Toovey (eye) and Martin Bella (hip) during the match further depleted the team.

Lyons responded to the added responsibility of captaincy with arguably one of the finest games of his career. 'I'm still filthy about the Canberra semi-final,' says Cliff who, considering he played in over 300 games for the club, surprisingly remembers many of the game's details. 'It was a high-scoring match but "Ridgey's" goal kicking kept us in the hunt. Canberra led 28-14 early in the second half but we were able to put two tries on and we trailed by two points. With minutes remaining, John Jones was injured and then penalised by (Bill) Harrigan for interfering with the play-the-ball. We were still appealing to the referee as we turned our backs to help 'Jughead' from the field when Mal Meninga quickly tapped the ball forward and sent Gary Coyne over for the try. Coyne scored four tries that day, I'll never forget it.'

Canberra won 34-26, in a match that cost the defending premiers incredibly. While the Raiders defeated Norths in the preliminary final before failing to Penrith in the grand final – its star players, Daley and Stuart, shackled by their injuries, several Manly players were selected for the Kangaroos' train-on team for the up-coming 15-day tour of Papua-New Guinea. This was the first time Australia had undertaken an extensive tour of the fledgling rugby league nation. Cliff was subsequently named in Australia's 20-man squad along with clubmates Martin Bella and Geoff Toovey. 'I was happy to get a call-back after the being dropped for the deciding State of Origin match but I was just as glad "Tooves" was recognised for his great season,' Cliff says. 'He was certainly one of the toughest guys I played along side of.'

The Kangaroo Tour of Papua-New Guinea at the end of 1990 was plagued by injuries from the beginning. Penrith's grand final heroes, Mark Geyer and Greg Alexander, were chosen but pulled out because of injury, as did Canberra pair Ricky Stuart and Laurie Daley. During the tour Steve Walters, Craig Salvatori and Andrew Gee were forced to return home while Kerrod Walters, Mark McGaw and Steve Roach joined the squad mid-tour as replacements. The luckless Roach was then replaced by former Balmain team-mate Bruce McGuire after he broke his ankle in his first match.

Cliff appeared in all five games on tour, including both Tests, 'That tour was a real eye-opener,' he says. 'The hotels we stayed in were great but once you went out to the games, it was like another world. People living in huts, half-naked. But wherever we went, we were mobbed – even in the highlands.'

Australian coach Bob Fulton concedes that it was one of the toughest tours he had to take away in his decade as national coach. 'We were certainly looked after – we stayed in good hotels and trained in a compound with a lot of security,' Fulton says. 'The only real problem we had on tour was the enthusiasm of the people. The people up there really love their football. They absolutely idolised Mal (Meninga) and Cliffy and were in awe of the big men, Mal and Glen Lazarus and Steve Roach.'

Australia opened the tour with a 40-6 win over Central Zone at Lae. Coming off the bench, Cliff scored one of Australia's eight tries in a match that was played in oppressive heat. Sweltering conditions again greeted them on the island of Rabual with the Kangaroos defeating Islands Zone 42-25 after being met by an enthusiastic opposition much more accustomed to the stifling heat. Islands Zone led 13-10 in an even first half until Brisbane winger Willie Carne set up a try for Cliff. By half-time, Australia led 26-13 and extended its lead by another ten points before wilting in the heat.

Cliff was Geoff Toovey's halfback partner in the First Test at Goroka, replacing incumbent Test pivot, North Sydney's Peter Jackson, who had been injured in the second match of the tour. The Australian team took full advantage of the cooler conditions to run in 12 tries to nil against the Kumuls. Lyons scored the second try of his Test career in a match that could easily have produced a record international score had Mal Meninga and Gary Belcher been successful with all 12 shots at goal. Papua-New Guinea had no answer to a bigger, stronger Australian Test team and were soundly beaten 58-2.

Cliff's view that Papua-New Guinea was 'another world' was highlighted in the Kangaroo's fourth match, against Highlands Zone at Mount Hagen. Safety on and off the field was the main concern in the modest 28-3 victory - the Australian players distracted from their task when riot police fired tear-gas into the excited crowd of 9000 and sprayed gunfire above the heads of the locals trying to break into the ground. On the field, the Australian players were hit in a number of high tackles with the game turning spiteful in the second half. To cap a remarkable day, play was stopped when tear-gas wafted across the field and the players were forced to lie on the ground and given wet towels to cover their faces.

Bob Fulton remembers the match vividly. 'We knew that the match at Mount Hagan was going to be hard - they were a small but willing side. Unfortunately, they sold more tickets than they had space for and there were just as many people outside the ground as inside. You have to remember that some of these people had trekked for days to get to the match and were obviously disappointed not to be able to see their heroes. It got a bit scary because even though we were not in any real danger, having to hit the deck midway through a match was something that you didn't have to confront on a daily basis back in Sydney.'

Australia wrapped up its mini-tour with a 40-6 win in the Second Test at Port Morseby. Cliff made way for the return of Peter Jackson but made his appearance from the bench. The match in which Willie Carne scored his second consecutive Test hat-trick proved to be Cliff's final appearance in the green and gold. 'A lot of people would think that a Test jersey against the Kumuls wouldn't mean as much as a Test spot against Great Britain, but to me each of my Test jerseys mean the same,' he says. 'It's in the record books that I played in six Tests and I valued every moment I got to wear the jersey.'

In October, Cliff returned home in time to celebrate his 30th birthday with his wife and family. For many professional rugby league players, age 30 signifies veteran status – the twilight of a player's career. But in Cliff's case, he was just getting started. Although the curtain would fall on his representative career the following year, incredibly, he would play for another eight seasons.

CHAPTER TEN

Changes

The years between 1992-94 brought a number of changes in Cliff Lyons' career and in his personal life. In 1992, the year the Lyons' celebrated the birth of their third child, Cliff made the last of his representative appearances with back-to-back appearances for City Firsts and City Origin. Manly failed narrowly to make the semi-finals that year and prior to the start of the 1993 season Graham Lowe suffered a recurrence of the health problems that had hampered his coaching career and was forced to stand down from the club. Lowe was replaced by the man who had taken the Sea Eagles to their last premiership title - Bob Fulton, the club's favourite son and the incumbent national coach. Under Fulton's guidance in 1994, Cliff captured his second Gold 'Dally M' Award as 'Player of the Year'.

For Cliff and Karen Lyons, the early 1990s were a time for family - raising three young children at the family home in Dee Why. Daughter Gabrielle was born in September 1992 six weeks premature as was the case with each of Karen's children. There were more now important things in their life other than football and Karen Lyons especially noticed subtle changes in the game and in the way a player like Cliff was valued.

'For a time, I think the game stopped being fun for Cliff. (Manly coach) Graham Lowe became very intense after his illness and the players were concerned for his health. It was a stressful time for everyone. Manly always did well and there was always high expectations in the club – now there was just such a tense feeling if they lost.'

1992 was a lean all round year for the Manly club. For the first time in State of Origin history, no Manly player was selected for the New South Wales team. Then, for the first time since 1964, no Manly player took part in the domestic Test series played against Great Britain. Cliff played in all 22 matches that year but, after a poor start to the season and an apparent lack of depth in the club, Manly was bundled out of semi-final contention when it lost its final three matches of the season.

The Sea Eagles won their opening two matches of the competition, against Gold Coast and Canberra, before slumping to lose six of its next eight matches. On April 12, the Sea Eagles crossed the Tasman to take on Newcastle in the first premiership match played outside of Australia. A crowd of 17,268 packed Carlaw Park to watch the match, a prelude to the mooted inclusion of a New Zealand club into the NSWRL. The Knights, boasting several Kiwi players, defeated Manly 16-13 in a thrilling match. Soon after, Auckland was admitted into the 1995 competition, beating bids from Wellington and Melbourne.

After a solid start to the 1992 season, Cliff was selected as pivot in City Firsts after being overlooked for City Origin duty with selectors opting for in-form St George utility, Brad Mackay. After playing a full match for City Firsts, Cliff was then used as a reserve for City Origin, replacing former Australian Wallaby and Irish Rugby Union international Brian Smith at halfback. If there was any irony in the fact that for the first time in the 66-year history of the annual fixture that Country won both matches, then Cliff – a 'bushy' who had masqueraded as a City-dweller for his entire professional career, failed to see it. Cliff was just too much of a professional to stomach two losses on the same night.

The Manly team was approaching something like its 1991 form in the middle part of the year, strengthened by the return of its injured personnel and the ability of its star players to overcome injuries without the added pressure of appearing in the State of Origin series. Lowe, who was again battling health problems and had vacated the Queensland State of Origin coaching position in favour of Wally Lewis, was able to get the best out of his charges. By the time Manly defeated Newcastle in its return match in Round 19, it had a tenuous hold on fifth position.

However, the Sea Eagles lost their grip on a semi-final berth when it went down to premiership front-runner Brisbane 22-10 at Lang Park. Needing to defeat Illawarra, placed ahead of them on the ladder, Manly was given added incentive by the impending retirement of captain Michael O'Connor and the fact that the Illawarra match was to be his last game at Brookvale. 'We desperately wanted to send Mick out a winner,' says Cliff. 'We played ourselves into a winning position, leading 8-4 with a minute remaining, but we panicked. We tried to close it up before it was over.' The Steelers' representative winger Rod Wishart dashed through a gap between Cliff and O'Connor and scored under the posts to give the Steelers a 10-8 win after the conversion.

Any hope of a semi-final position was dashed in the last round loss to Cronulla, 28-8. It was clear that Lowe did not have the ammunition to undertake a realistic premiership assault and he was the first to admit that the established players had performed below their best. At the end of the year, Michael O'Connor retired, Test prop Martin Bella left for Canterbury and Kevin Iro vacated the club after two mixed seasons.

Towards the end of the year, Manly signed a five-year deal with

Pepsi worth $4 million. Gone was the familiar dark maroon and white pin-stripped jersey that had been synonymous with the club for two decades. The club's playing strip was replaced by a predominately white jersey with lighter areas of maroon and blue that made the players look conspicuously like the product they were sponsoring. Former Manly premiership-winning and Australian Test coach Frank Stanton returned to the club to take over the role as Chief Executive from the ailing Doug Daley and the timing of Stanton's return was to prove crucial, especially in light of the illness to Graham Lowe.

In January 1993, Manly travelled to Auckland for a trial match amid a highly publicised week of public engagements designed to capitalise on the Kiwi club's entry into the NSWRL competition. The club's premiership campaign was rocked by two injuries - a broken jaw suffered by newly appointed captain Geoff Toovey and a knee injury to Cliff. The dejected pair travelled back to Australia earlier than the other players to receive medical attention and took no part in the Coca Cola World Sevens competition in which Manly was defeated by Easts in the final, 18-12.

On February 22, Graham Lowe finally made the difficult decision to resign because of ill health. 'We knew that Graham was sick but when he was hospitalised, we still didn't see his resignation coming,' says Cliff. 'We were used to the disruptions his illness caused but we started worrying more about Graham's health than about winning and I think that showed in the results on the football field. "Bozo's" return proved to be the best thing for the club's stability and Manly's three grand final appearances (1995-97) prove that.'

Bob Fulton who had retained ties with the club in his role as coaching director and although he was the logical choice as Lowe's replacement, he thought long and hard about taking on the role. 'It wasn't something I sought, more a case of stepping back in because it was needed,' Fulton told me. 'I was national coach at the time and had media commitments to consider, so I listened to the advice of people I respected. I spoke to Ken Arthurson at the ARL and to my employers at 2UE. But basically, I took it on because I knew that the club was in good hands with Frank Stanton as Chief Executive. Frank and I had been through a lot together – we had played together, Frank was then coach of the side that won the 1976 grand final and I was captain, and then we went away with the Ashes-winning 1978 Kangaroos with me as captain and him as coach. The club had the leadership to be successful.'

After the disappointing results of the 1992 season, Fulton was well placed to guide the Sea Eagles through the rebuilding phase that was needed to take the club back to the semi-finals. Interestingly, only Cliff, Darrell Williams (who took next to no part in the 1993 season) and Des Hasler remained from the club's 1987 premiership-winning team. During the season, Fulton would use young backs Jack Elsegood, Danny Moore, John Hopoate and Chris Ryan as well as rookie forwards Nik Kosef and Steve Menzies. A serious knee injury to Matthew Ridge would see local junior Ivan Cleary stamp his reputation as a goal-kicking fullback. Elsegood's great form saw him win the 'rookie-of-the-year' award in 1993 while Cliff was to form a marvellous partnership with Steve Menzies the following year.

'I had seen Steve Menzies coming through the Manly juniors in the early 1990s when he was a centre at Harbord,' says Cliff Lyons. 'He made his first grade debut during 1993 and after we got to know each other the following year, we formed a natural combination. Steve knew where the gaps were and how to run through them and I knew how to get the ball to him at the right time.'

Starting the year without the services of Toovey and Lyons, Fulton chose Des Hasler to captain the club in its 19-4 win against Norths. The Sea Eagles fielded a young and inexperienced side and quickly found a winning formula, thrashing Souths (30-10) and Illawarra (23-2) in consecutive weeks. Cliff made his return from injury in the club's Round 4 victory over Newcastle, and backed up the following week in the close 14-8 win against the Gold Coast.

Manly suffered losses against Easts, Parramatta, Canterbury and Canberra in April before regrouping to win 11 of its last 12 matches. The only loss in the second half of the competition being a narrow 21-20 loss to St George. During this period, Geoff Toovey captured the five-eighth position with Cliff being used from the interchange bench. When Toovey suffered a knee injury in the Round 19 match against Newcastle, Cliff regained the pivot role for the club's run to the semi-finals.

Coming off the interchange bench was somewhat foreign to Cliff, who had been used as a starting player for his entire career and had relished the opening clashes that traditionally commenced a match. Cliff came off the bench in eight of his eighteen matches in 1993 and it was a trend that was to become increasingly frequent in his later career. While Cliff agrees with Bob Fulton's belief that the interchange rule actually lengthened his playing career, he says, 'I think coming off the bench also affected my tackling. 'I had built my early reputation, especially in the bush, as a solid defender and really enjoyed that role but once I started coming off the bench, it was to organise the attack and I didn't have to do as much defensive work.'

Manly ultimately finished in fourth place in a highly competitive premiership table. Just two points separated the final five teams with Canterbury heading the list on 34 points followed by St George (34), Canberra (33), Manly (32) and Brisbane (32). The Sea Eagles faced the unenviable task of taking on defending premiers Brisbane in the sudden-death minor preliminary semi-final, with the Broncos looking to win the premiership from fifth place for the second year in succession.

Fifteen minutes into the semi-final, Cliff suffered one of the most painful injuries he has experienced in his grade career. 'I damaged a rib cartilage in a tackle and had to leave the field immediately,' Cliff says. 'I couldn't breathe it was so painful and there was no chance of me even running let alone making another tackle.' Brisbane was ruthless in its defeat of the Sea Eagles, racing to a 20-0 lead after 27 minutes before running out easy winners, 36-10. The Manly defence was simply not good enough and for the second time in his coaching career, Fulton realised the club would have to buy a number of class players in order to win the premiership.

Two veteran Sea Eagles who felt the squeeze of the club's pursuit of new players were Des Hasler and Cliff Lyons. Hasler saw the writing on the wall and accepted a one-year deal to play with Hull in England before returning to the club in 1995. For Cliff, who was still under contract in 1994, negotiating what could have been the final contract of his career proved to be a difficult task. After using a succession of managers, it was just Cliff and Karen who negotiated with Frank Stanton towards the end of his career – their bargaining tools being Cliff's undeniable talent and the goodwill his career had generated at the club. It also didn't hurt that Cliff won the Gold 'Dally M' Award the week before he came to terms with the club.

The newly promoted Western Reds sounded out Cliff about going to Perth for their foundation season in 1995. '(Reds coach) Peter Mulholland spoke to us many times during 1994,' remembers Karen. 'He was a really nice guy and it sounded like things were really set up for Cliff if he was to go to Perth. In the long term though, it was loyalty to "Bozo" (Fulton) that kept us here. "Bozo" said "I want you to stay at Manly" and for Cliff, that was enough. In hindsight, staying with Manly also extended Cliff's career - especially when you look at what happened to the Reds.'

For Cliff, the mere fact that Bob Fulton valued his services enough to make him part of the club's future plans, was enough to re-sign a two-year contract at the end of 1994. Fulton's standing in the game, and his position as national coach, drew three players who were to have a significant impact on the fortunes of the Manly club in the 1990's. Mark Carroll, whose career at Souths had stalled since his 1990 Kangaroo tour, joined Manly with the express purpose of furthering his representative career. David Gillespie and Terry Hill joined Manly from Wests following the fallout over the departure of coach Warren Ryan.

Manly opened the 1994 season in the best possible fashion with an emphatic win in the Coca-Cola World Sevens. With Cliff Lyons at the forefront of the Manly attack, the Sea Eagles won five consecutive matches culminating in the 44-12 thrashing of St George in the final. There was the potential embarrassment of the Pepsi-sponsored Sea Eagles claiming the Coca-Cola Trophy and NSWRL officials ordered the Manly players to remove their sponsors' caps when they mounted the stage to accept their awards. For the second time in his career, Cliff was named 'Player of the Competition'.

One of the real success stories of the 1994 season was the emergence of free-running second row forward Steve Menzies, a teenager who had garnered good press in several interchange appearances the previous year before suffering a knee injury. Menzies scored 16 tries in 1994 (the most by any forward in the history of the Manly club) with the great majority set up by Cliff Lyons. 'Steve's a natural runner; great on his feet and very nimble,' says Cliff. 'There was no conscious positioning on our part, it was something that happened naturally. The trick was hang on to the ball until the last possible second, suck in the opposing defence, and then get the ball to him. Steve did the rest.'

Selected to tour with the Kangaroos at the end of the season, Menzies went on to top the try-scoring lists in the ARL the following year. By 1999, Menzies had become only the second forward (behind

South Sydney legend Bob McCarthy) to score 100 career tries and it would be fair to say that Cliff Lyons has given the final pass in most of those tries. Following Cliff's return to the game in 1999, Newcastle coach Warren Ryan went one step further, stating that Lyons has probably set up more tries than any player in the history of the game. Considering that, at the time of writing, only three other players have joined the '300 game club' – Terry Lamb, Andrew Ettingshausen and Paul Langmack, it is hard to argue with this statement. Lamb and Ettingshausen were among the game's best finishers while Langmack's latter career was dogged by injury.

Manly started the 1994 season with a 26-20 loss to Canterbury at Brookvale Oval with Fulton moving Cliff to halfback and Matthew Ridge the unusual choice of five-eighth. That partnership lasted only one game although Cliff retained the halfback role in the 18-all draw against Illawarra in the following match. The Sea Eagles then handed Wests a monster of a thrashing, 66-8 – the biggest winning score posted by a NSWRL team since Manly thrashed Penrith (70-7 in 1973). The Sea Eagles led 36-4 at half-time with Cliff controlling the game in the second half. Manly scored 11 tries and 11 goals that day with Cliff bagging a double. A Cliff Lyons field goal sealed Manly's 13-10 win over Newcastle in their next match, a contest that started the ferocious series of duels between rival forwards Mark Carroll and Paul Harragon.

'"Spud" Carroll was an asset to the club in the mid-1990s,' says Cliff. 'He had a real passion for the game and was good at motivating the forwards, especially before a match. He'd be in their ear, reminding them what had to be done out on the field but once out in the middle, he'd be the first one taking the ball up.'

The Sea Eagles suffered losses to Cronulla and Canberra either side of a lacklustre 28-13 win over Souths. The Rabbitohs led 11-4 but when halfback Craig Field was sent off, the battling club had the disappointment of former players Mark Carroll and Terry Hill scoring late tries to win the match. Accounting for Penrith, 28-18, Manly commenced an eight-match winning sequence that produced the some of the most emphatic wins in the history of the club.

Manly disposed of Brisbane 21-11 at Brookvale Oval with Cliff sealing the win with a try and a field goal. In the match against Norths, which drew a record crowd at North Sydney Oval, Cliff potted a late field goal to give Manly an 11-8 win. The Sea Eagles then handed out a record 42-0 loss to Balmain at Leichhardt Oval before staving off a late comeback from Parramatta to run out eventual winners, 32-18. Even when Manly had an off day, as they did against the Gold Coast in their next match, Cliff pulled out something extra – setting up tries for Toovey and Cunningham before he scored the clincher to give his club an 18-14 win.

St George suffered its worst defeat in the club's 73-year history when it fell victim to Manly, 61-0. The Sea Eagles scored a dozen unanswered tries in the romp that brought superlatives from the Sydney press. Author David Middleton wrote in 1994's Official Rugby League Yearbook, '32-year-old five-eighth Cliff Lyons masterminded the massacre with a variety of attacking options that left Saints bamboozled.' At the midway mark of the season, Cliff was leading virtually every best and fairest competition and playing arguably the best football of his career. Cliff's confidence was at a peak and the fact that he was chosen in the starting line-up in every match in which he played that season had a lot more to do with this than people realise.

A hat-trick to Steve Menzies was the highlight of the 34-0 thrashing of Easts in the club's next match, the Sea Eagles scoring a combined total of 95 points to nil in consecutive matches. Although the bubble burst against eventual minor premiers Canterbury in the next match, the Sea Eagles won the following five games by an average score of 33 points to 13. However, an anomaly in the way the competition was structured in the 1990s meant that teams did not play each other twice during the season. Without that 'level playing field', Manly still needed to defeat eventual premiers Canberra in the final match of the season to cement a vital place in the top three.

A bumper Brookvale Oval crowd saw Manly fail to convert a 6-all score-line into a much-needed win. Canberra led 21-6 before the Sea Eagles posted two late tries. The 21-18 loss relegated Manly to a sudden-death play-off against Brisbane. Manly lost to Brisbane in similar circumstances in 1990 and 1993, and history was to repeat in the first elimination match of the 1994 semi-final series. Almost a year to the day since the Broncos thrashed Manly 36-10, Brisbane used all its defensive prowess to defeat the Sea Eagles, 16-4. Manly trailed 6-4 early in the second half but after failing to crack the Brisbane defence, fell victim to two late tries.

Cliff received some consolation with his naming as Gold 'Dally M' Player of the Year. The presentation of the prestigious award which is sponsored by News Limited gave an insight into the media organisation's perilous relationship with the NSWRL at the end of the 1994 season. Gone were the days of glitzy nights at the Entertainment Centre. The award was handed out by Channel 9's Peter Sterling and ARL Chief Ken Arthurson in a low-key, pre-match ceremony an hour before the playing of the semi-final against Brisbane - just the sort of distraction a player needs before a big match.

One of the reasons Cliff re-signed with Manly in 1994 was because of the lure of a second Kangaroo Tour at the end of the year and he realised that leaving the club might harm his chances of selection. Following Cliff's second Gold 'Dally M' win, he started wondering if this was a good omen for selection with the Kangaroos, as had been the case in 1990. Eight Manly players were added to the train-on squad for the Kangaroo Tour – Geoff Toovey, Cliff Lyons, Owen Cunningham, Danny Moore, Terry Hill, Ian Roberts, Mark Carroll and Steve Menzies.

Despite Bob Fulton putting forward good cases for the selection of all the Manly players, selectors ultimately chose only three on the tour - Ian Roberts, young forward Steve Menzies and centre Terry Hill. Geoff Toovey especially, can be considered desperately unlucky not to have been chosen but nobody had a better case than Cliff Lyons. The champion five-eighth had been voted the best player in the competition and his non-selection for the Kangaroos was a huge disappointment to both he and Karen - Cliff deserved to be on that tour and he personally felt cheated. It is interesting to note that more than half of the players chosen on the tour showed their loyalty to the ARL by joining *Super League* the following year.

'Cliff played the entire 1994 with a hernia problem,' admits Karen Lyons. 'When he didn't go away with the Kangaroos at least now he could get it fixed.' While the 18th Kangaroo squad to tour Great Britain and France retained the Ashes with a hard-fought 2-1 win in the Test series, Cliff celebrated his 33rd birthday in Manly Hospital recovering from a hernia operation.

In November, ARL Executive Chairman Ken Arthurson returned to Australia before the deciding Third Test of the Anglo-Australian series to hold urgent talks with News Limited executives after it was leaked that the media organisation planned to mount a rival competition called *Super League* in 1995. It was to be the start of a three-year war that was to turn the game of rugby league on its head.

CHAPTER ELEVEN

ARL v. the Super League

For the first time in three years Manly's senior players, including Cliff who had fully recovered from his hernia operation, were on deck for the club's pre-season trials, Tooheys Challenge and World Sevens competitions. On January 20, 1995, Des Hasler marked his return to the club by scoring two tries in the 18-6 win over the Sydney Bulldogs (formerly Canterbury-Bankstown) in a trial at Carlaw Park, Auckland. In the words of coach Bob Fulton, Manly fielded a mobile '90s style' pack of forwards and put all of its attacking capabilities on show in the 36-12 win over Fiji in the final of the Coca-Cola World Sevens.

But the 1995 season, which culminated in one of the most controversial matches in the history of grand final contests, was completely overshadowed by the code's attempted take-over by News Limited, the media organisation owned by expatriate Australian billionaire Rupert Murdoch. On February 6, the ARL's 20 clubs signed a five-year loyalty agreement after rival media baron

Kerry Packer, who held exclusive television rights of the game, threatened to sue any club which breached its obligations with the ARL and went over to the proposed rebel competition. While this settled the issue in the short term, news of an impending *Super League* coup would just not go away.

On April Fool's Day 1995, News Limited announced the signing of key players from Canberra, Cronulla, Western Reds, North Queensland Cowboys, Brisbane and the Sydney Bulldogs. Despite the rejection of a *Super League* franchise by Newcastle (followed by Norths and later St George), the ARL was then effectively isolated on the international stage when the New Zealand and Great Britain Leagues joined *Super League* on April 6. On May 13, News limited offered Manly the tenth franchise in the rebel competition.

Ken Arthurson, the then Executive Chairman of the ARL, was in the eye of the storm. 'I told Manly quite categorically at that time that whatever decision they made - whether to stick with the ARL or to go with News Ltd, was a matter for them to decide,' he says. 'I stressed to the club that under no circumstances should they personally feel obligated to me or to my stand against News Ltd. The club needed to make its own decision, which it did.' Although the Manly club rejected the *Super League*, News Ltd targeted individual players within the club and some took the bait.

Matthew Ridge and Ian Roberts both signed *Super League* contracts, as did Owen Cunningham later in the year. Although Ridge and Roberts became outspoken critics of the ARL's administration of the game, their stance did not affect the Manly players. Says Cliff of that period, 'We just worried about the football side of things and concentrated on what we did best – which was playing the game.' Cliff was also approached by *Super League* and following news that Graham Lowe was taking over the North Queensland Cowboys as interim coach in 1996, his name was linked to the fledgling club.

'Cliff could have signed with *Super League* and set himself up for life,' says his wife Karen. '*Super League* was interested in him playing with the Cowboys, although it was never definitely stated which club he would play for. They offered a three-year deal – a lot of easy money, but once again the concern was that Manly might fall apart if it lost players like Cliff, Des (Hasler) and "Tooves". When you have had such loyal support from the club and there are friends like Bob (Fulton) and Frank (Stanton) at the helm that you respect, how do you look those people in the face and say, "So long I've got a better offer?" You can't.'

Manly put the code's off-field drama behind it in the most emphatic fashion by winning the first fifteen matches of the season. At the halfway mark of the premiership, there was talk that the Sea Eagles may even emulate the deeds of the great St George team of 1959 and go through the season undefeated. Ultimately, Manly lost only two of twenty-two competition matches during the year on its way to capturing the minor premiership. The club scored 687 points in 1995 and conceded only 248. Steve Menzies headed the try-scoring table with 21 tries, just in front of team-mate John Hopoate, while Matthew Ridge topped the point-scoring list, setting a club record total of 257 points for the season.

'To dominate the competition in the three years the *Super League* war was going on is a credit to the Manly club and to its players,' says Bob Fulton. 'At the beginning of the 1995 season, "Gus" Gould (Sydney City and NSW coach) and myself were receiving faxes on a daily basis, from here in Australia and in Great Britain, in order to sign up players and undermine the *Super League* competition and its internationals. It was a huge distraction from being able to focus purely on rugby league but the Manly players in particular were great.'

Approaching 34 years of age, Cliff enjoyed a remarkable season in 1995. He started in each of the club's 25 matches and finished second in final polling for the Gold 'Dally M' Award for 'Player of the Year'. On August 23, 1995 Cliff celebrated ten years of service with the club with a privately organised Testimonial Dinner at Manly-Warringah Rugby League Club. Acknowledged Manly-Warringah fan, Booker Prize winning author Thomas Keneally, has always been a keen supporter of Cliff's and the pair have always greeted each other with a warm 'Mate!' when they meet. Keneally wrote an open letter to Cliff to mark the occasion:

"All of us who enter 'Brookie' or other grounds in hope on any weekend have always heard someone around us say, 'If Lyons plays well, Manly will play well.' What a compliment that is to your range of skills, the stuff you take for granted but which amazes us punters in the stands! They know anything can happen, and attack can develop anywhere and move anywhere. Sure, they groan sometimes at a loopy Lyons pass in front of the goal mouth, but if you didn't have the guts to do that, you wouldn't have the guts to do half the unpredicted, mad, unorthodox, stylish, classy and exhilarating things you do."

While Manly sailed unchallenged at the top of the league table, Canberra, Brisbane and Cronulla – each a *Super League* aligned club, gained a top four position while Newcastle, St George, the Sydney Bulldogs and Norths fought out the elimination quarter-finals. The Bulldogs regrouped after an inconsistent season to qualify in sixth place in the eight-team semi-final series. The *Super League*-bound Bulldogs had been floored by the decision of four of its leading players – Dean Pay, Jason Smith, Jarrod McCracken and Jim Dymock, to renege on their hastily signed News Ltd contracts and switch their allegiance back to the ARL.

The Bulldogs gained some much-needed premiership momentum with semi-final wins over St George and Brisbane before exacting revenge for their 1994 grand final loss against Canberra with a 25-6 defeat of the Raiders in the first of two preliminary finals played.

Manly on the other hand, hot-favourites to win the club's first premiership in eight years, was not as impressive in its wins over Cronulla and Newcastle. The Sea Eagles were uncharacteristically flat in attack and reticent in defence and it was only several glimpses of brilliance from Cliff and Geoff Toovey that saw Manly make the grand final.

In the first quarter-final, between Manly and fourth-placed Cronulla, the Sharks led 20-8 midway through the second half before Cliff sent his shadow Steve Menzies in for a try. The Sea Eagles still trailed 20-18 with nine minutes remaining with the Sharks' chief playmaker, halfback Paul Green, continuing to look dangerous with a late break. 'I knew Paul Green had something on for his outside backs and so I decided to run up on him really quick,' Cliff remembers. Green rushed the pass and Cliff intercepted to send winger Craig Hancock on an uninterrupted run to the try-line to give Manly a 24-20 win.

Despite finishing first on the premiership ladder, the 1995 semi-final series meant that Manly had to face Newcastle in a sudden-death preliminary final in order to qualify for the grand final against the Bulldogs a week later. In heavy conditions, Manly led 6-4 with 15 minutes remaining after Cliff and Steve Menzies had been heavily marked by the Newcastle defence. It was left for Manly captain Geoff Toovey who, having led the way in defence during the entire match, set up the winning try for his appreciative five-eighth. 'Close to the Newcastle try-line "Tooves" ran crossfield to create the gap and turned the ball inside to me,' says Cliff. 'I sailed through and slid over for the try beside the posts. As I scored, I looked up into the crowd and saw a sea of Manly fans so I gave them a salute.'

The image of a beaming Cliff Lyons, his hand raised in appreciation of the supporters, is one of the best portrayals of the almost symbiotic relationship he enjoyed with the club's fans during his 15-year career.

The eight-team semi-final series meant for the first time in the history of rugby league play-offs that there was just a one-week break before the playing of the decider with no actual benefit to the minor premiers. 'In the 1995 grand final, we weren't ready mentally,' admits Cliff. 'The match came up on us too quickly – grand final week came and went, and our lead-up to the match went very quickly. Before we knew it we were out there on the field and then it was all over. Some major things went against us in that match but we didn't play well enough to overcome them.'

After the ARL banned those referees who had signed *Super League* contracts, a group which included Bill Harrigan, Graeme Annesley and Stephen Clark, David Manson and Eddie Ward were the main contenders to referee the grand final. Against most expectations, veteran Queensland referee Eddie Ward ultimately gained the job. Of the subsequent series of errors, in which Ward awarded a try to Steven Price after a forward pass from Jim Dymock, allowed a try to Glen Hughes on a seventh tackle, and awarded a try to Rod Silva after a forward pass from John Timu, Bob Fulton says;

'We got a referee from left field. It was not just that these things happened but more the timing of those events that brought us undone. However, having said that, we did not play well and there was no use us whingeing after the match, especially considering that we were an ARL club and Sydney Bulldogs was *Super League*. A seven-tackle try had never happened before in a grand final – the only other instance I can remember is in a semi-final in 1978 between Manly and Parramatta and people still talk about it! Hardly anyone in the media jumped up and down about us losing the grand final in those circumstances.'

There was little tension in the opening minutes of the grand final with two early penalties giving the Bulldogs good field position. Halligan's first penalty kick at goal from 40 metres out was unsuccessful but then Terry Lamb, the veteran Bulldog pivot and captain, was sin-binned for tackling Matthew Ridge while running back from an off-side position. 'Matthew always backed himself when he saw a chance to come into the front line of attack and he had two players on his outside. Had he not been tackled illegally, Manly would have scored for sure,' Cliff says.

It was just the type of professional foul for which Lamb had become notorious during his career and the tough little pivot was met by a barrage of abuse from the Manly players. 'Lamb was cunning like that,' says Cliff of his opposing pivot whose 300-game career mirrors his in more ways than one. 'I always had a good duel with Terry when we played against each other. We were very similar players in how we were built and in how we approached the game.'

Ridge's goal took Manly to a 2-0 lead but the Sea Eagles could not capitalise on Lamb's enforced absence from the field and this was to be the only time that they led in the match. Jim Dymock kicked early in the tackle count with the Bulldogs' content on defending against Manly deep in the Sea Eagle's territory. Following Lamb's return in the 16th minute, fiery Manly winger John Hopoate was penalised for punching his tackler while in possession and Halligan's goal tied the scores at 2-all.

The first try in the match came mid-way through the first half. Terry Hill lost the ball just outside the Manly 22 metre line and several rucks later, Dymock charged at the Manly defensive line and got an around-the-corner pass to Simon Gillies that was clearly forward. The Bulldog prop found rookie forward Steven Price in support and gave the pass for the first contentious try of the match. 'Under pressure we dropped too much ball in our own half,' Cliff admits. 'We knew the pass was forward straight away but once it was on the scoreboard you couldn't do much about it.

Sydney Bulldogs coach Chris Anderson used an effective double-pivot tactic, with Lamb and Dymock standing either side of the ruck, and instructed Gillies and Lamb to double mark Cliff and Nik Kosef at every opportunity. 'The Bulldogs had obviously done their homework and targeted the playmakers in the team,' Cliff says. 'Lamb was rushing up on me all match while Ben Gillies moved up to cut off the short pass. They were offside for most of the second half and frustrated us.'

Just before half-time, two great five-eighths came face-to-face when Lamb gathered Cliff's chip-kick in the shadows of the Bulldogs' goal-posts. A short time later, Gillies was penalised for lying on the Manly players in the tackle and Ridge's penalty goal narrowed the half-time scores to 6-4. Early in the second half, these spoiling tactics forced Manly into making several errors. The Sea Eagles struggled to carry the ball out of their own half and were met by a Bulldog pack that had caught a sniff of victory.

The passage of play that ultimately decided the grand final came after a relieving penalty put Manly back onto the attack. Kosef broke through the Bulldog defence and made a long sweeping run toward the SCG corner before passing to winger Craig Hancock. In a great covering tackle, Jason Hetherington, John Timu and Darryl Halligan bundled Hancock into touch with the try-line in sight. The ensuing scrum, which allowed the Bulldogs to regain possession, resulted in the most controversial moment of the match.

The tackle sequence after winning the scrum – Halligan, Silva, Newton, Pay and Polla-Mounter, brought the Sydney Bulldogs up to the halfway mark. Sensing that it may be the last tackle, Lamb went to first receiver and feigned to kick before firing out the pass to Dymock. Following a wide pass from Dymock, Ryan scooted up-field only to be tackled short of the line. Depending on which way you look at it, Lamb then either conned the referee into thinking there was another ruck remaining or merely played to the referee's whistle, and scooped the ball up from dummy-half and lofted a pass to the waiting line of attack. The ball moved quickly out to

Dymock, Silva and Pay, whose overhead pass found replacement centre Glen Hughes unmarked in the back-line.

The Channel 9 commentary team later alluded to the fact that Ward may have erred but in fairness to the referee, it was not confirmed until after the match that the try had been scored on the seventh tackle. Although this mistake could not be blamed for Manly's loss, it is hard to disagree with Bob Fulton's assertion that it came at a crucial time in the match. Halligan missed with his conversion attempt and the Bulldogs only led 10-4 with twenty minutes remaining before Lamb extended this by a further point with a field goal eight minutes later.

Poor handling hampered Manly's attempts to get back into the match. Hopoate, Gartner and Carroll each gave away possession inside the final ten minutes but Manly certainly wasn't helped by some inconsistent decisions from referee Ward. In the final fifteen minutes of the match, Manly players were twice penalised for being inside the ten metres and were continually having to back-pedal. With three minutes remaining, Sydney Bulldogs' former All-Black centre, John Timu, ran the ball on the sixth tackle and stepped inside the tired Manly defence. His pass to fullback Rod Silva again appeared to be forward but by then the game was well and truly lost. Halligan's conversion completed an unanticipated 17-4 victory while Manly's kick-off to restart play summed up the team's performance on the day - it went out on the full.

It was left for Terry Lamb to accept the last Winfield Cup, before completing an emotional victory lap that saw him meet with his family on the eastern side of the oval. For Cliff, the opportunity to complete his own lap of honour of the SFS in front of his own cheer squad would have to wait. 'The Bulldogs played well and deserved their victory. It was a tough way to learn but we came back a much better team the following year.'

On November 19, and with the battle over control of the game looming in the courts, Kerry Packer announced that Channel 9 had secured the free-to-air rights to all the *Super League* matches. 'As a result, the ARL found themselves at the mercy of a power battle between two media organisations,' says Ken Arthurson, 'and those two media organisations finally got together and made a business deal that left us out on a limb. In retrospect, if I had my time all over again I would have tried to get Channel 9 to share its television rights which is what Murdoch was after in the first place. I don't know how I could have tried any harder than I did, but Kerry Packer was adamant that under no circumstances would he give any of the free-to-air or Pay TV rights to News Ltd, and the ARL had a legally binding agreement with him.'

'But quite apart from that legally binding agreement we had a moral obligation to stand by the agreement. At the end of the day, Kerry made a business decision to televise the *Super League* series. The decision was obviously personally disappointing - it was the beginning of the end for us. Had I known that this was going to happen, I don't think I would have been as morally obligated as when the issue first came up at the end of 1994. We at the ARL sincerely believed - and I still believe that no business organisation should control sport, particularly if that organisation *is* the media. I just think it's morally wrong. Sport belongs to the people.'

Super League changed things - the game was now just a business. Today, rugby league players may be viewed as 'elite athletes' worthy of huge financial rewards, but they are also products that are expendable. The game that says to State of Origin hero Billy Moore, Test rake Jim Serdaris or Melbourne's grand final try scorer Craig Smith that there is no longer a place for them in rugby league - despite the fact that each player hasn't even reached the age of thirty, could never again accommodate a career like the one Cliff Lyons enjoyed.

CHAPTER TWELVE

Premiers Again

On February 23, 1996, Justice Burchett handed down the decision in favour of the ARL declaring that the loyalty agreements signed the previous year were valid and binding for all 20 premiership clubs to the ARL until the year 2000. While News Limited quickly launched its appeal in order to kick-start its rebel *Super League* competition, it was business as usual for the ARL in the 1996 season.

Manly's results that season speak volumes for Bob Fulton's ability to galvanise the talent in the club in the face of the continuing distraction of the *Super League* war and Australia's growing isolation from the international rugby league stage. Fulton had the onerous task of lifting his players after the disappointing loss to the Bulldogs in the 1995 grand final. 'We had two ways of looking at it,' Fulton says. 'Either we could go downhill or go up another notch and in my mind we climbed the mountain again. Manly's 1996 team was a very good football side. We had a great defensive record – better than any other side in the history of the game.'

After an uneasy start to a season delayed by court action, the Manly club celebrated its fiftieth year by winning 21 of 25 matches played (undefeated at Brookvale Oval) on the way to capturing the club's sixth premiership title. The Sea Eagles scored 609 points during the year and conceded just 213 points - 8.5 points per match. For the second year in succession, Steve Menzies topped the club's try-scoring list, crossing for 20 tries, while Cliff, the veteran five-eighth, appeared in every match of the year (20 matches and five games from the bench).

'It was amazing the difference twelve months can make,' Cliff adds. 'We were a maturer team for the loss against the Bulldogs and got to know each other's play a little better. Having lost a grand final, we were committed in 1996 not to go through that again. The newer players at the club – Terry Hill, David Gillespie and Mark Carroll, certainly weren't hard to motivate. We had lost one grand final - now they wanted to win one badly.'

Lyons was granted permission from Manly to captain the Aboriginal 'Dream Team' in the Coca-Cola World Sevens on February 2-3 at Parramatta Stadium. While St George declined to release star teenager Anthony Mundine, the 'Dream Team' contained established first graders Ken McGuinness and Nathan Blacklock. The team was organised by David Liddiard, the former utility back with Parramatta and Penrith who had been a team-mate of Cliff's at Manly in the early 1990's after returning from England where he had played for Hull.

'Cliff resurrected my career in Australia,' says Liddiard. 'At Parramatta, I had great success running off Mick Cronin and had always been taught to follow the ball-players in a club. At Manly, that man was Cliff Lyons and I quickly became his 'black shadow'. It was interesting to see Steve Menzies do pretty much the same thing as soon as he came into grade.'

After his retirement, Liddiard started National Aboriginal Sports

Corporation Australia; their brief to nurture the 'sporting talents of Aboriginal and Torres Strait Islander people, especially those in remote rural communities, and to use this as a springboard to greater success in education, employment and career development'. As CEO of NASCA, Liddiard is answerable to a board of high-profile business people including former Federal Minister for Sport John Brown, high-profile radio commentator Alan Jones, Aussie Home Loans' John Symond, and former Prime Minister Bob Hawke.

'I first went to Colin Love with the idea of fielding an Aboriginal "Dream Team" in the 1996 World Sevens and the ARL Board gave us the green light,' David recalls. 'We were sponsored by Rio Tinto which paid for our jerseys and covered our training costs. Cliff Lyons was captain-coach and I knew straight away that he would do a great job. He was highly respected by all the players and led by example. At training Cliff did everything – the goal kicking, kicking for touch, organising the play. The crowd support we got at Parramatta Stadium was fantastic but not surprising. The Koori Knockout competition that is conducted each year is always well supported and whenever we go to country communities to conduct coaching clinics, the response from people is great.'

The 'Dream Team', which played in flashy red, yellow and black jerseys modelled on the Aboriginal flag, proved to be extremely competitive and a popular hit with the hardy crowd of which had come to watch the 24-team competition despite the withdrawal of the *Super League* clubs. 'I was the runner for the team,' says Colin Lyons. 'To be involved in that team with Cliff was fantastic because that dream had been coming for such a long time. People had been talking about an Aboriginal team in the ARL since I was a kid.'

The 'Dream Team' defeated Melbourne and the USA in its group to advance to the quarter-finals of the Cup Competition. In a stunning upset, Cliff's charges defeated Easts 12-10 while Manly was beaten by Norths at the same level. Although falling to Norths in the semi-final, 28-16, Cliff's direct involvement in the Aboriginal team proved to be one of the most satisfying achievements in his career. At the end of the year, David Liddiard organised the first All Aboriginal rugby league Tour of Great Britain.

Colin Lyons adds, 'Cliff doesn't have to go out and promote his Aboriginality - just being Cliff Lyons is enough. Without consciously knowing it or promoting it, he is a role model for others and being in the "Dream Team" and wearing that jersey helped do that for him. However, at times I think there was some influence on him not to have so much involvement in teams outside of Manly and that was fair enough because of his career and his contract.' Bob Fulton says that the Sea Eagles gave Cliff some freedom during his later career because of the years of service Cliff had given but that this was 'ultimately to the club's detriment.' With the 'Dream Team' finishing ahead of Manly in the 1996 Sevens, the club banned Cliff from playing in the team the following year.

Manly opened its season with a 44-6 thrashing of Souths at Brookvale Oval. However, *Super League*-aligned players held firm at first and refused to return to the field, and with their clubs refusing to pull them back into line, the stand-off resulted in six forfeited matches in the first round of competition. Auckland (the only *Super League* club prepared to field a second grade team), Newcastle, South Queensland, Parramatta and St George benefited with two points from the forfeits (the first time this had happened in League since the infamous 1909 final between Souths and Balmain) before the court ruled that the players were in breach of the original decision and that they were to return to their clubs and to play in the ARL competition.

Despite the court's ruling, the *Super League* issue continued to fester during the season. In June, eight players - Laurie Daley, Glen Lazarus, Brett Mullins, Andrew Ettingshausen, David Furner, Steve Walters, Steve Renouf and Wendell Sailor, refused the Australian

Test jersey because the NZ representative side chosen wasn't a ratified team selected by the Super League-backed NZRL. For a player like Cliff who valued the Australian jersey like gold, it was hard to fathom that any player would turn their back on the chance to represent their country.

Matthew Ridge, who had already returned to New Zealand in anticipation of playing for Auckland in the proposed *Super League* competition, chose to sit out the early part of the season until finally returning to his former club in Round 9. No doubt the media portrayed Ridge as a symbol of the split in the code after he left Australia and was quoted as having less than flattering opinions concerning how the ARL was running the game. Ridge, a guaranteed match-winner, was welcomed back by the premiership favourites. 'We were happy to have Matthew back,' says Cliff without the slightest hint of emotion, 'he was worth ten points a game to us.'

Manly and Easts battled for the position of premiership front-runners for much of the season before the Sea Eagles eventually captured their second successive minor premiership. St George, the most improved team in the latter part of the season, qualified for the semi-finals on the strength of the great form of halves Noel Goldthorpe and Anthony Mundine. In anticipation of *Super League* commencing its competition, the son of former Australian boxing champion Tony Mundine had trained with the Sydney Bulldogs in the 1995 off-season before reluctantly returning to St George. He then signed a lucrative contract mid-year to play with the Brisbane Broncos but returned to the Dragons at the end of the 1997 *Super League* season. In April 2000, Mundine turned his back on his career in rugby league, citing racism and a lack of respect by representative selectors as his main reasons for pursuing a career in boxing.

Although some comparison can be made in the careers of the two five-eighths, the similarity between the game's two highest-profile indigenous players of the 1990s ends at their public personas. Cliff – the quiet tradesman, a consummate team player and professional. Mundine – the outspoken individualist and non-conformist, 'The Man'. Says Cliff of rugby league's lost soul, '"Choc" (Mundine) certainly puts a lot of pressure on himself to perform each week but he's the type of guy who wears his heart on his sleeve and that's just the way it is with him. I respect him for that.'

St George defeated Canberra, 16-14 in its elimination semi-final match, while Manly accounted for Sydney City 14-12 in an equally controversial qualifying semi-final. The Sea Eagles then qualified for its second successive grand final with an authoritative, 24-0 shut-out of Cronulla in the preliminary final. Manly led 6-0 at half-time after Cliff came into play, ran crossfield, held up the ball and scooted over a try in the 22nd minute. Manly frustrated the Cronulla attack in the second half, forcing fullback David Peachey into making several errors that resulting in tries to Steve Menzies and Danny Moore.

Norths' quarter-final victory over Brisbane revived the club's hopes that 1996 was the year it would win its first title since 1922 but the Bears were soundly out-gunned by an enthusiastic St George team in the first of the two preliminary finals played, 29-12. 'St George was attempting to "do a Canterbury", coming from the bottom end of the semi-finals but we weren't going to take our opposition lightly, not like the year before,' said Cliff.

The Manly team that took the field on grand final day had undergone some significant changes from the side that had lost to the Bulldogs twelve months before. Coach Bob Fulton again elected to play his veterans, Lyons and Hasler, from the interchange bench alongside former Wests and St George forward Neil Tierney and experienced club winger Craig Hancock. Former All Black and Leeds centre Craig Innes secured the centre position alongside Terry Hill with Australian representative centre Danny Moore on the wing.

For the second successive year, fullback Matthew Ridge had to overcome a fitness test to take his place in the grand final after suffering a serious bout of concussion in the preliminary final, while captain Geoff Toovey took the field with a broken eye socket.

'Jimmy Serdaris also gave us a lot more go forward that we didn't have the previous year,' Cliff observed. After a slow start to the season, the former Wests and 1994 Kangaroo hooker had secured a first grade spot with talented ball-playing forward Daniel Gartner grabbing his place in the forward pack following the loss of Ian Roberts. Roberts had elected to sit out the remainder of the season to recover from a knee injury before linking with the North Queensland Cowboys in 1997. Bob Fulton elected to keep Nik Kosef at five-eighth to partner captain Geoff Toovey. 'It was "Bozo's" idea to use Nik as the starting five-eighth,' Cliff says. 'I wasn't happy about it but "Bozo" was the coach and I wasn't going to argue with him. It was hard not starting the game – every player likes to run out and start a grand final, but with the unlimited interchange rule it was just something I had to deal with in my career.'

'The interchange rule probably lengthened Cliff's career by several seasons,' Fulton counters. 'I had him off the field because I didn't want him in there doing the tackling because the opposition forwards would run at him and tire him out. When Cliff came into the attack, I wanted him fresh.' Fulton concedes it would have been hard for veteran players such as Cliff and Des Hasler – players who had come through their careers playing a full 80 minutes of football, to sit off at different stages of the match – especially the opening ten minutes of a grand final.

A heavy downpour during the pre-match entertainment resulted in the grand final being played in slippery conditions. The match was just minutes old when Manly captain Geoff Toovey proved his fitness with a finely-judged kick behind the St George defence. Craig Innes and John Hopoate led the chase for the ball with Innes touching down for the first try of the match. Ridge's conversion gave Manly a 6-0 lead which was extended a further two points in the 16th minute after the controversial fullback landed a penalty goal in front of the posts.

Midway through the first half, Lyons came into the attack with Fulton using the veteran five-eighth judiciously throughout the match whenever the Sea Eagles were in possession. 'It was hard at first coming onto the field and having to get into tune with everyone else who had been on the field for twenty minutes or so and were already warmed up,' he admits. 'But I learned quickly and adjusted my game.' In the 25th minute, as Cliff prepared to receive the ball, he saw the St George defence rushing up on him and batted his pass onto Matthew Ridge who was standing behind in support. Few players would have either the skill or the courage to do that in a match let alone in a grand final.

When Lyons took the field, Manly looked more assertive and self-assured. Sydney City and former NSW Blues coach Phil Gould, who was part of the Channel 9 commentary team, could sense the change in the Manly attitude. After Cliff found touch with a 30 metre clearing kick, Gould exclaimed, 'Last year they (Manly) turned up hoping Canterbury would let them play. This year they've turned up with their football boots ready to play.'

Wayne Bartrim put the first points on the board for St George in the 37th minute after Owen Cunningham was penalised for stripping the ball from his opposite number Tony Stone. From the restart of play, a minute before half-time, Matthew Ridge put in a short kick after noticing that St George utility forward Nathan Brown momentarily had his back turned. As Ridge pounced on the ball and quickly jumped to his feet, Brown had the barest of holds on him - his finger wrapped inside the collar of the Manly fullback's jersey. Referee David Manson was unsighted, later ruling that in his opinion Brown had no effective hold on Ridge, and allowed play to go on. Ridge surged forward while the stunned St George defence held off waiting for Manson to blow his whistle.

With Ridge pulled down metres from the try line, Steve Menzies crashed over beside the posts from the next play-the-ball, injuring his right thigh in the process. 'Being a former "rah-rah", the short kick-off was a ploy "Ridgey" sometimes used,' Cliff says. 'There was no doubt that Brown had a hold on him but it was on the ref's blind side and he didn't see it. This was just that little bit of luck that we needed and considering what happened to us against the Bulldogs the year before, it might have been the little bit of luck that was owed to us. In sport you make your own luck and Matthew backed himself. The referee said play-on and you always play to the whistle.'

Ridge's conversion took the Sea Eagles to a commanding half-time lead, 14-2, effectively placing the match beyond St George's reach. The Dragons had struggled to stay in touch with Manly in the first half but not even a passionate on-field complaint from St George captain Mark Coyne had a hope of changing the scoreboard. Most post-match reports criticised Manson's decision but the first-time grand final referee was adamant that he had made the correct decision.

In the second half, the Sea Eagles remained solid against a resolute St George attack that was growing in confidence. Cliff Lyons took the field in the 45th minute but two minutes later, he was back on the bench after Manly was forced to again defend. However, the memory of the previous year's loss to the Bulldogs was enough for the Manly players to counter any hope of a St George fightback. Despite losing Ridge and Menzies in the second half (both players were off the field injured during late periods of the match), Manly put the contest beyond doubt when Moore crossed in the corner after good lead-up work from centre Terry Hill. In Ridge's absence Innes converted from a wide angle to take the Sea Eagles to a commanding 20-2 lead.

Lyons did a lot of sweeping in defence, cleaning up several speculative kicks from the St George players in the vital period midway in the second half. If there is one incident that exemplifies Manly's resolve in defence, it came in the 58th minute of the game. After receiving an accidental elbow to the head when tackling Wayne Bartrim, an injured Cliff Lyons momentarily remained on the ground. Terry Hill physically stood over the veteran five-eighth, yelling at him to get up and get back into the defensive line. Not only did Cliff will himself to get up off the ground, he ducked behind the Manly defence in the next passage of play to gather in Noel Goldthorpe's kick into the in-goal area.

'That's what grand finals are all about!' remarked Channel 9 commentator Peter Sterling, who certainly should know. The former Parramatta halfback still bristles at the memory of Canterbury hooker Mark Bugden scoring the winning try of the 1984 grand final while Sterling's team-mate Ray Price lay on the ground injured.

With 20 minutes remaining, Nick Zisti got outside the cordon of Sea Eagle defenders and scored in the corner. Bartrim's great sideline conversion brought the gap between the two teams to within twelve points but given Manly's defensive record during the year, realistically the chance of a grand final upset never looked likely. Spurred on by captain Geoff Toovey, Manly were not to be denied the premiership this time. Toovey was awarded the Clive Churchill Medal at the end of the match and capped this honour by captaining Australia in a one-off Test against Papua-New Guinea at the end of the year.

Mark Carroll should have scored in the 62nd minute but he lost control of the ball as he crashed over under the posts. Jim Serdaris showed his immense value to the team when he made a long, determined run with ten minutes remaining. With Cliff back on the field, the veteran pivot showed the perfect timing that marked his career by positioning himself so that he could field St George captain

The classic passing style of
Cliff Lyons.
(Courtesy Manly Daily)

Celebrating Leeds' Yorkshire Cup Victory, 1988-89. Fellow Australians Sam Backo and Andrew Ettingshausen (partially obscured) are pictured while Cliff holds the 'Player of the Match' trophy.

While playing for Leeds in 1988-89, Cliff was selected for 'Rest of the World' vs. UK. Captained by his former Norths team-mate Mark Graham, other Australians pictured include Noel Cleal, Sam Backo, Michael O'Connor, Gavin Miller, Dale Shearer, Allan Langer and Steve Ella. It is hard to tell Cliff and Kurt Sorensen apart!

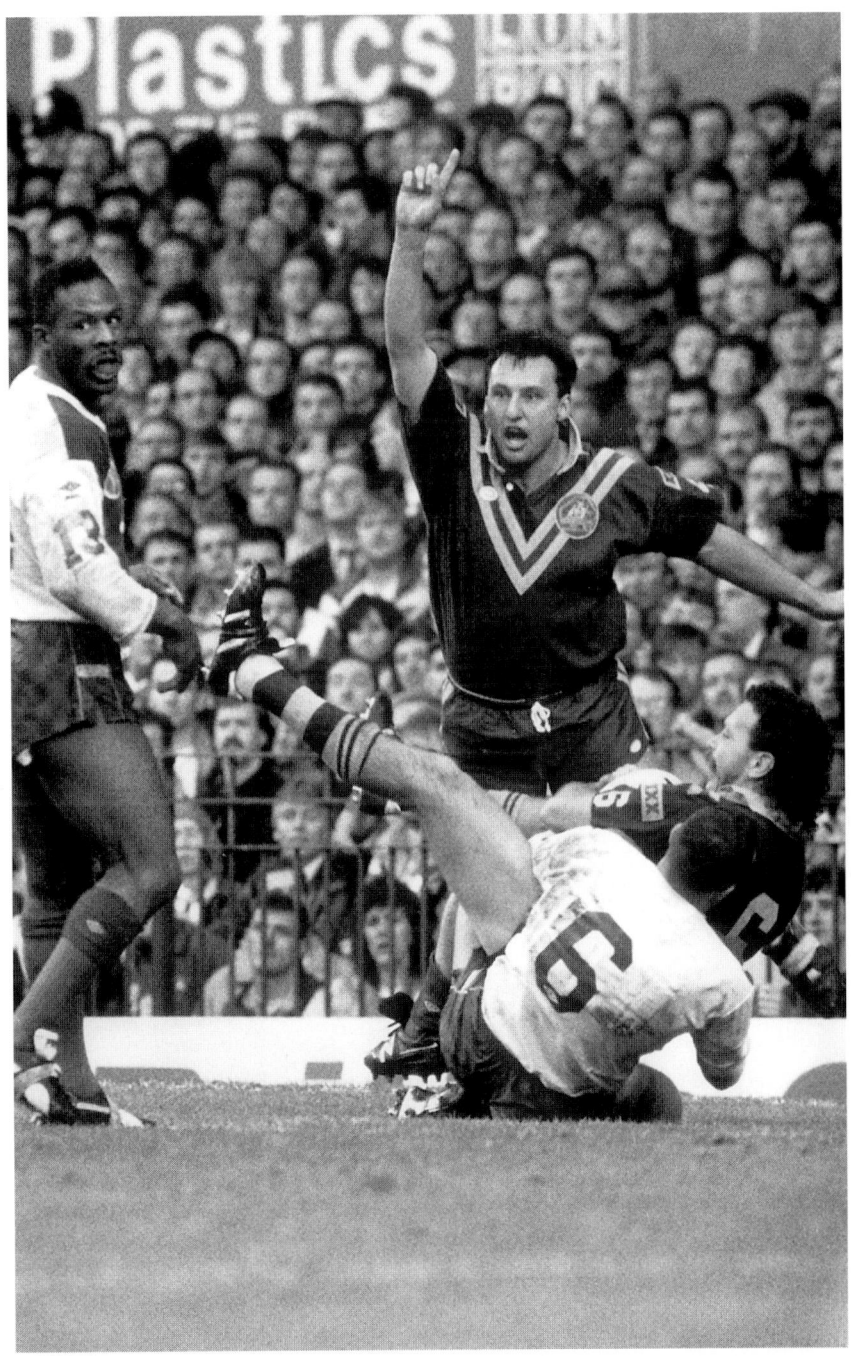

Cliff Lyons scores Australia's second try in the Second Test against Great Britain in 1990. Note the contrasting faces of Laurie Daley and Lions captain Ellery Hanley

That winning grin...

(Courtesy Manly Daily)

Saluting the crowd after scoring a try against Newcastle in a semifinal, 1995.

(Courtesy Manly Daily)

(Courtesy Manly Daily)

Cliff waving to his family on the Hill at Brookvale Oval after scoring a try against Illawarra.

(Courtesy Manly Daily)

Cliff and Manly captain Geoff Toovey after the club's 1996 Optus Cup win.

Premiership number 2, 1996.

(Courtesy Manly Daily)

A tearful farewell... with Chief Executive Frank Stanton making a presentation at Manly Leagues Club, 1998.

(Courtesy Manly Daily)

Back with the Sea Eagles - waiting on the bench, 1999.

Farewell to Brookvale Oval.

Mark Coyne's kick and be tackled with the ball as the full-time siren sounded.

For Cliff, the euphoria of the club's Optus Cup win was as real as his first in 1987 although strangely, the club waited until two months later to hold a parade along Pittwatter Road to celebrate their success. Manly's second premiership title under the direction of Bob Fulton brought obvious comparisons with the club's 1987 team. Fulton says diplomatically, 'It's hard to compare sides from different eras because you have to compare the opposition in the context of the competition. Put it this way, both the 1987 and 1996 sides were great sides in their own right and worthy premiers.'

Winning the grand final, enjoying a lap of honour with his team-mates and celebrating with his family and friends would have been a good way for Cliff to finish his career. David Gillespie and Des Hasler had played their last games for the club in the grand final (although Hasler later decided to have one more season with Wests) but Cliff desperately wanted to play on and see out his career at Manly. News that the club had signed halfback Craig Field from South Sydney for the 1997 season meant that it would once again be difficult for Cliff and wife Karen to negotiate a contract.

'Cliff always settled his contracts with the club on a handshake,' says Karen Lyons. 'That's the way they did business – on trust. Cliff is very loyal and while thoughts of following the "big money" at another club did come up, for Cliff to leave Manly felt like leaving family.' It was at times disappointing then, that rather than reward Cliff's loyalty, Manly continued to recruit players who had no real regard for club.

'I think Frank (Stanton) was trying to suggest to us that Manly was making other plans for the future and that it was time for Cliff to retire,' says Karen. 'Towards the end of their careers most players have been given the whisper by their club - but then Cliff never believed in making it easy for anyone. There was a copy of the club's 1996 Annual Report on Frank's desk for his approval and on the cover was a photo of Cliff superimposed over the Sydney Football Stadium, bursting through. I don't think we were meant to see it but Frank and I noticed the picture at almost the same time.'

The thought of Manly without Cliffy? Impossible! By the end of the meeting, Cliff Lyons and the club had agreed to a further two-year deal.

CHAPTER THIRTEEN

Three into Two Doesn't Go

On October 4, 1996, the Federal Court over-turned Justice Burchett's ban on the rival *Super League* competition. With the success of News Limited's appeal, rugby league fans faced the prospect of watching two separate competitions in 1997. By its very nature the season was the most divisive in the 90-year history of the code in this country. The ARL ran its traditional competition comprising ten teams – Balmain, Gold Coast, Illawarra, Manly, Newcastle, North Sydney, Parramatta, St George, South Queensland, South Sydney, Sydney City and Western Suburbs, while *Super League* conducted its rebel competition with ten teams vying for the Telstra Cup. While the *Super League* premiership fuelled the fears of many rugby league loyalists – that it was a competition instigated by Brisbane for the benefit of Brisbane, the ARL grand final between defending premiers Manly and Newcastle produced one of the most exciting and controversial matches ever to decide a premiership.

'I want to say a little as possible about that grand final,' admits Cliff who, in the years since the game was played had refused to watch a replay until it became necessary for the preparation of this book. 'In my mind and the minds of a lot of the other Manly players, that game is tainted. On the day, there was nothing between the two teams and the final result could have gone either way. The Knights just kept coming at us and produced that little bit extra to score a late try and win the match. But some Newcastle players were later found to have taken drugs – and that's something those players have to live with.'

Super League clubs were not involved in the Coca Cola World Sevens in 1997, the rival organisation conducting a World Nines competition (in which Australia lost the final to New Zealand) in Fiji from January 31 to February 2. Although Canterbury released its talented winger Hazem El-Masri to play for Lebanon in the ARL knockout, Manly declined to release Cliff for the Aboriginal 'Dream Team'. The Sea Eagles lost both its matches and was relegated to the Plate competition while the 'Dream Team' defeated Papua-New Guinea (26-10) and New Zealand (16-14) before narrowly losing to Norths in the quarter-final of the Cup competition.

The Sea Eagles sorely missed the consistency of Matthew Ridge's goal-kicking during the year, the talented fullback playing for Auckland in the *Super League* competition. Although boosted by the signing of Souths halfback Craig Field, the inability of the club to settle on a halfback combination would come back to haunt it at semi-final time. At the end of the season Manly captured its third successive minor premiership but the rotation of the halves, the increased speed of the play the ball, and lapses in defence created reservations about the Sea Eagles' chances of defending the premiership.

The move to Manly obviously proved to a difficult one for Craig

Field but Cliff had a lot of time for the young halfback. 'Craig had a good attitude - he was desperate for success but he was frustrated by the way he was used at Manly. Basically, we had three halves at that time and three into two doesn't go. Craig was often trying to play two roles during a game – halfback and five-eighth, and part of the problem was the club tried to mould him into something he wasn't. He was certainly a talented player - impulsive at times but very passionate about his game. Sometimes he tried too hard and made mistakes. It was self-deflating – he'd make a mistake, cop a "raspberry" from the crowd and then get the hook from "Bozo". The Brookvale Oval fans didn't warm to him but they certainly didn't see the best of Craig Field.'

From having their best defensive record in history, 1997 proved to be disappointing in comparison. The Sea Eagles could score points – Terry Hill topped the try-scoring list with 22 tries and was supported by John Hopoate (15), Steve Menzies (13) and Craig Innes (12), but the team conceded 416 points in 25 matches. Part of the problem was changes to the policing of the play-the-ball area designed to take advantage of the ten-metre defensive rule and make the game a quicker spectacle. Ricky Stuart, Cliff's 1990 Kangaroo Test partner, was especially critical of *Super League's* interpretation of the ruling that was threatening to turn the game into 'touch football'.

But even at the beginning of the two competitions, there was some movement towards peace and a resolution of the conflict that had raged for two years. Ken Arthurson and John Quayle both resigned from their administrative positions with the ARL in the hope of securing a commitment for a unified competition, with national coach Bob Fulton also publicly stating that he was prepared to stand down if this would hasten the process. Throughout the year there were destabilising stories in the press that Manly and Easts would defect to *Super League* at the end of the year or that a merger with Norths was on the cards, but at the time both rumours were denied.

Although Manly were undefeated after the opening seven rounds, the Sea Eagles lost 'easy matches' against Balmain, Wests and the Gold Coast and recorded high-scoring draws with Illawarra (34-all, an ARL record) and the Gold Coast (24-all). The highlight of the premiership season was the club's 34-24 win over Easts after being down 18-0. The low-point - when Norths exacted some revenge against its proposed merger partner in handing Manly a 41-9 thrashing at North Sydney Oval.

The ARL competition conducted a 'final seven' play-off series with Manly defeating the Mal Reilly coached Newcastle in Game 3 of the second-round of preliminary semi-finals. The Knights were without the services of Andrew Johns and Robbie O'Davis but the Sea Eagles had to overcome a determined forward pack to record a 27-12 win. In what was becoming an all-too familiar scenario, Mark Carroll was knocked unconscious after colliding with opposing forward Paul Harragon. 'Mark Carroll and Paul Harragon were like magnets on the field,' remembers Cliff. 'Somehow, they always managed to find each other and line each other up.'

The try to John Hopoate just before half-time proved to be the turning point in the semi-final with Manly proving its superiority in the final 15 minutes of the match. With the scores locked 12-all, the former World Cup representative winger took great delight in running over the top of opposing winger Darren Albert. Manly coach Bob Fulton had persevered with the Nik Kosef/Geoff Toovey halfback partnership to start the semi-final before calling on Cliff after the opening ten minutes of the match. When Kosef was subsequently suspended for the following match after being cited for a dangerous tackle to Matthew Johns, Fulton moved Toovey to five-eighth and promoted Craig Field to halfback for the preliminary final against Easts.

The move proved to be prophetic, with Field piloting Manly into the grand final with a late field-goal with three minutes remaining. Manly led 8-6 at half-time after fullback Shannon Nevin landed four penalty goals but, sparked by young lock Anthony Colella, the Sea Eagles extended their lead to 16-8 after tries to Innes and Menzies. Former Manly winger Jack Elsegood scored the try that brought Sydney City back into the match before Scott Gourley's try equalised with seven minutes remaining. Field's one-pointer, on the back of his best match since coming to the club, ensured that he remained at halfback for the grand final. Manly lost Jim Serdaris in similar circumstances to Kosef after he was suspended for a dangerous tackle. However, the minor premiers were clear favourites to win back-to-back premierships with Newcastle having lost each of its eleven previous encounters against the Sea Eagles.

On grand final day, Cliff came off the bench wearing the Number 9 jersey with Toovey at Number 6 and Field Number 7. 'It was ploy by "Bozo" to put doubt in Newcastle's mind about who was starting the game,' says Cliff. Young utility forward Anthony Colella was used as acting dummy half with Field, Toovey and Cliff alternating between halfback and five-eighth.

The match opened with a caution to Newcastle captain Paul Harragon for a high shot on Toovey, a tackle that saw Mark Carroll come storming in. When Field failed to find touch in the second minute of game, Newcastle was on the attack on the halfway mark. In the first scrum of the match, Toovey stood in the centres in defence with Fulton electing to bring Craig Innes closer to the scrumbase. Soon after, Harragon was penalised for his second high tackle but then executed a stunning, ball and all tackle on Carroll who lost possession when he groggily got to his feet and incorrectly played the ball.

Andrew Johns missed an early shot at goal that would have settled the nerves of the Newcastle camp. In the seventh minute of play,

Steve Menzies seemed hard done by when he was deemed to have knocked on when playing the ball but Manly won the ensuing scrum against the feed - unheard of in the modern game, and was back in an attacking position. Kosef, acting at five-eighth, switched play and Field's cut out pass resulted in Innes sending winger John Hopoate over in the left-hand corner.

Hopoate, who positioned himself outside his opposite number Darren Albert, was clearly elated with the effort and celebrated by grabbing the head of Robbie O'Davis and cheering in his face. In response to Hopoate's annoying habit of sledging his opponents after scoring a try, Cliff says, '"Hoppa" is a pretty quiet person off the field but when he got pumped, that's how he chose to express himself. It's an individual thing, part of his personality. He may have gone over the top sometimes but in his defence, he was a player who copped his share of sledging, especially during his junior career. He was a Tongan playing in the Manly juniors and he copped heaps. That tends to rub off on some players and put them in a reverse situation, you would give it back in shovel loads.'

Fullback Shannon Nevin's great kick from the sideline gave Manly a 6-0 lead after 9 minutes. Minutes later, Field found good distance with his clearing kick but the ploy of having Toovey standing in the centres came undone when the fearless Manly captain was wrong-footed and fell into the attempted tackle of rampaging Newcastle winger Adam MacDougall. The burly winger's thigh caught Toovey in the head and the Manly captain collapsed as he tried to make it to his feet. Toovey's exit from the game with concussion was an unfortunate cue for Cliff Lyons to come off the bench.

Shannon Nevin magnificently fielded a high kick under his goal posts and Steve Menzies turned defence into attack with a fifty metre run, but the early clashes started to take their toll. Daniel Gartner received a nasty gash over his eye and Field had to be carried off by the Manly trainers after injuring his ankle. O'Davis almost scored after Shannon Nevin took his eye off an in-goal kick while five minutes later, Andrew Johns almost stole a try down the right flank only to be pulled back short of the line in a desperate tackle by John Hopoate.

Manly's second try, scored in the 23rd minute, was the result of a classic piece of blindside play by the champion Sea Eagles backline. Seven pairs of hands handled the ball in the attacking rush down the left-hand flank with Toovey, back on the field after recovering from concussion, handling three times, and Cliff Lyons and Craig Innes handling twice in the movement. The former All Black centre touched down and Manly led 10-0 after Nevin missed with the conversion from wide out.

Field returned to the match after receiving a pain-killing injection to his injured ankle. Newcastle turned up the pressure late in the first half. Danny Moore was caught in-goal in an Andrew Johns' tackle before Hopoate was bundled into touch while fielding a Matthew Johns chip-kick. From the ensuing scrum – with Cliff packing down in the second row and Toovey standing in the centres, Newcastle fullback Robbie O'Davis produced a brilliant 'in and away' that completely wrong-footed Toovey and Manly centre Terry Hill. After diving over for the try in the left hand corner, the Newcastle fullback did a victory dance to celebrate with Andrew Johns' conversion taking the score to 10-6.

Just when the Knights seemed to be getting back into the match, Harragon was hit in a monster tackle by Mark Carroll which forced loose the ball on the 20 metre mark. Two minutes before half-time Toovey, Field and Lyons combined to send Nevin over for a try. In what had become a trademark of his game, Lyons ran crossfield and he deftly passed the ball to Nevin who had instinctively positioned himself on the inside. 'With the sliding defence a lot of coaches used, the inside ball always picked up the lazy defenders who struggled to come across,' says Cliff. 'When I passed the ball inside, I didn't even have to look. I knew Shannon would be there.'

Nevin's conversion of his own try gave the Sea Eagles a comfortable 16-8 lead which they maintained until the break. Harragon and Carroll again clashed on the sound of the half-time siren with Toovey shadowing referee Manson all the way to the tunnel protesting about the number of high tackles in the match. Fulton also confronted Manson in the tunnel and was less than impressed with the referee's rulings on high tackles. 'The leniency showed by the referee disappointed me. It was open season and the Newcastle players were given a free reign,' says Fulton.

Early in the second half, Craig Field belied his injured ankle when he made a break, kicked toward Darren Albert's wing and tackled the Newcastle flankman in-goal. However, great defence from Newcastle pushed Manly back a further 25 metres. The ugliest incident of the match occurred in the 45th minute when Geoff Toovey was stomped on the face by MacDougall as he struggled to step out of the tackle to play the ball. Toovey took the full brunt of MacDougall's boot across the eye and nose and had to be assisted from the field to receive medical attention. While the Newcastle winger immediately went to Toovey's aid after realising what had happened, the damage was done. MacDougall was subsequently cited over the incident and suspended for three weeks.

Lyons again replaced his injured captain and was welcomed by a high, late tackle by replacement Newcastle forward Steve Crowe. Cliff came up swinging, disregarding his veteran status and mixing it with the youngster. Manly was awarded the penalty with Cliff cautioned by referee Manson for taking the matter into his own hands. In the 53rd minute Newcastle finished a perfect set of six tackles with Andrew Johns putting a well-timed kick into the Manly in-goal area. Although the kick was cleaned up, the ensuing drop-out goal created further problems for the Sea Eagles.

Manly had a chance to gather the ball on the 30 metre line but the linesman incorrectly ruled that Cliff had knocked on when falling on the ball. The veteran pivot passionately appealed to Manson the ball had come off his leg (replays support this) but the referee could not over-rule the touch judge and Cliff threw away the ball in disgust. From the next scrum, MacDougall was stripped of the ball and Johns kicked the penalty goal to reduce the gap to 16-10.

Paul Harragon was penalised for a third high tackle, this time clipping Nik Kosef, but Nevin missed the chance to extend Manly's lead when his penalty shot was wide. In the 68th minute Newcastle almost threw the game away after a Manly attacking rush (in which Cliff handled three times) ended with yet another kick to Darren Albert's corner. When Albert threw a wild pass in-goal to no-one in particular, Newcastle fans could have been excused for thinking the game was lost. Luckily, forward Adam Muir was on hand to clean up the ball in-goal. Following the goal-line dropout, Kosef had his pass knocked down by the enthusiastic Newcastle defence. From the ensuing set of six tackles, Newcastle powered downfield and it was only the last-ditch tackle from Craig Innes that stopped Muir from scoring.

Pressure is a funny thing, especially in grand finals. Leading by six points with nine minutes remaining, Craig Field kicked out on the full to give Newcastle great field position 40 metres out from the Manly line. Fortunately Knights' prop Tony Butterfield lost the ball and Manly was not directly punished for that mistake. Following a good run by Shannon Nevin, the Manly players set themselves for a field-goal to finally put the matter to rest. Field, who had taken Manly into the grand final with a pressure field goal the week before, was tackled with the ball on the fifth tackle. Nevin steadied himself behind a pack of Manly players to take the shot but Toovey, his head heavily bandaged, spied Cliff to his right. Although Nevin called for the ball, Toovey instinctively fired the pass out to Cliff who hurried his kick and watched it shave the right hand upright.

Manly was tiring noticeably and from the resumption of play on the 20 metre line, Muir, Jackson, Fletcher and Craigie took the ball deep into Manly territory. With seven minutes remaining, O'Davis danced around the tackle of Nevin and Carroll and flung his arm out to score under the posts. After being behind by eight points at the break, Johns' conversion tied the scores 16-all. The final six minutes of the game resulted in one of the most breathtaking finishes in grand final history.

In the 76th minute Matthew Johns failed with the first of three field goal attempts by the Knights before Manly gave away possession on the half-way mark after making good yardage upfield. If rugby league can be described as a game of percentages, then Field's flat pass to a heavily marked Nik Kosef was close to a zero. Kosef, who was clearly not expecting the ball, was hit in a tackle by Newcastle centre Mark Hughes and lost possession. Carroll and Harragon had their last piece of each other before Matthew Johns steadied for another shot at field goal. As the ball soared toward the uprights, Cliff stood dumbstruck underneath his goal-posts, hands on hips. For that moment, time had all but stopped.

'I remember watching the ball swing in the air,' says Cliff. 'I just stood there in awe of it.' The ball hung in the air for what seemed to be an eternity before the rebound snapped Cliff back into reality, and instinctively he caught the ball. The Manly players scrambled back into Newcastle's territory but on the fifth tackle, Cliff elected to run the ball and gave the pass to Hopoate rather than kick ahead. In fairness, there were no Manly chasers for a kick – all 26 grand final combatants were out on their feet.

With 79:30 gone on the clock, Andrew Johns tried for one, last, desperate field goal attempt from 35 metres out but his kick was charged down by Craig Innes. The rebound was fielded by Darren Albert who was tackled by Cliff and Mark Carroll on the right-hand side of the field. Johns, having failed with his kick, ran over to dummy half as Albert got to his feet to quickly play the ball. Running down the narrow blind-side past Cliff who was off-side, Albert loomed on Johns' inside as the rest of the Manly defence failed to come across. Evading the desperate tackle of Mark Carroll, the Newcastle winger took Johns' pass and sailed untouched through the gap to score under the posts.

There were just six seconds left to play. Newcastle had won 22-16.

'A game like that turns on its head,' says Cliff. 'I couldn't touch (Andrew) Johns because I was offside and I didn't want to be the one who gave a penalty away. We were trying to hang on until full-time so that we could regroup. The 1997 grand final was much harder than the semi-final we played against Newcastle the week before and was the toughest of the four grand finals I played in.'

Having a friend like Malcolm Reilly as the opposition coach didn't soften the loss for Bob Fulton who nevertheless is gracious in hindsight. 'Two weeks after the grand final we went away on a hunting trip and the game wasn't mentioned. You couldn't take it back. I felt we should've hung on – we had our chance. At the end of the day, if there had to be a winner other than Manly, I'm glad it was a mob like Newcastle who had stuck together during the *Super League* war and remained solid with the ARL. It was good for the city and good for the players.'

And how do players beaten in the final minute of a grand final even lift themselves off the ground? 'What *do* you do?' says Cliff, clearly exasperated at the mere mention of the match. 'What *can* you do? You console each other. You tend to look at the positives - we beat a lot of teams to even get there so you celebrate making the grand final. You thank the fans and all the people at the club who supported you during the year. You make the best of it - but there is a big hole left.'

That hole was partly filled in November 1997 when Cliff was inducted in the Narrandera Shire Sports Persons Hall of Fame. At a ceremony at Narrandera Ex-Serviceman's Club, Cliff Lyons, along with 24 others, was named in the Elite Sports Persons category who achieved national representation in their chosen sport. Included in the list was dual Wimbledon winner Evonne Cawley, legendary rugby league pivot Eric Weissel, Rugby Union Test players Jim Douglas and Jim Lenehan, and representatives from other sports such as shooting, equestrian and golf.

By December 1997, there was a renewed commitment from both league orgainisations to field a united competition involving 20 teams in 1998, reducing this to 16 teams the following year and finally 14 teams in the year 2000. But certain events immediately after the 1997 grand final took a lot of the gloss of Newcastle's premiership success. Two of the Knights' grand final heroes, Robbie O'Davis and Adam MacDougall, were subsequently suspended for 22 weeks each after random drug tests conducted in early 1998 produced traces of banned substances.

Cliff says finally in a bitter footnote, 'A couple of players got caught out because they took advantage of a time when the game was split and the powers that be weren't tough enough policing what the players were taking. It makes you wonder how many players, at any club for that matter, didn't get caught.'

CHAPTER FOURTEEN

Farewell

The 1998 season saw the code reunited under the newly formed National Rugby League banner but it was clear that the wounds of the *Super League*-ARL war would take a long time to heal. The mistrust and hurt was evident in the opening game of the season between Manly and *Super League* premiers Brisbane at ANZ Stadium, a match in which Manly captain Geoff Toovey and winger John Hopoate were sent off by referee Bill Harrigan for dissent. Recriminations reopened the Bob Fulton-Bill Harrigan feud, with allegations of bias against Manly by *Super League* forces. If that one match was any indication, the Sea Eagles were in for a tough year.

'1998 was always going to be hard, especially after losing the grand final the previous year,' Cliff admits. 'We lost a number of players; Mark Carroll and Danny Moore went to England, Dave Gillespie retired, Shannon Nevin went to Balmain and Craig Innes returned to New Zealand, but basically we didn't have the forwards to win the premiership.' Despite being joint-premiership favourites with Brisbane at the beginning of the season, Manly struggled for much of the year before a late-season fight-back saw the club snare the final place in the ten-team, semi-final series.

With Cliff increasingly used from the interchange bench in 1998, it appeared that his career was finally winding down. Midway through the year, he was informed that he would not be offered a contract in 1999. 'It was a "Catch-22" situation,' said Bob Fulton. 'We wanted to protect Cliff because Frank Stanton and I had seen too many players go for one season too long. The problem was, if it was left up to Cliff, he would still want to play – he just loves the game so much. And so, we gave him the send-off he deserved.'

On August 16, in the match against North Queensland at Brookvale Oval, Manly fans prepared to say goodbye to 'Cliffy'. Manly won the match 28-12 with Cliff starting the match as five-eighth partner to Craig Field. After the match, Cliff was given a rousing reception as he completed a lap of honour. 'We always sat under the scoreboard at Brookvale Oval,' remembers Karen. 'The Brookvale Oval fans grew to know us. Cliff's mum's has a bad back and while there was an area in the grandstands where the players wives could sit it was still in the weather. There were bars across the front of the stand and it was unsafe for the kids so we found a spot on the hill and made it our own little place.'

For the first time since the heady days of the 1996 grand final celebration, the auditorium of Manly Leagues Club was packed with a cheering, appreciative audience which gave Cliff a loud ovation when he took the stage. Unbeknown to Cliff, and in consultation with Karen Lyons, the Club prepared a special video entitled 'Cliffy' which highlighted his remarkable career. When Karen and the kids tagged on their own special message at the end of the tape, the tears flowed easily. 'Geoff Toovey gave a lovely speech at Cliff's "first farewell", basically saying the club should let Cliff play for as long as he wants,' recalls Karen. It was sentiment shared by many.

Colin Lyons and the rest of Cliff's family were also there that night. 'Karen and mum knew there was going to be a tribute to him at the ground after his final match but as far as I know, he didn't know the video was going to happen,' says Cliff's brother Colin. 'When he went up on stage and they showed that video of his career, there were tears in his eyes. He didn't want to let it go. Seeing him retire in 1998 was sad because I think Manly put him out to pasture too early. He still had something to offer. He wasn't ready then and he's still not ready.'

Manly defeated Auckland in its last premiership match, but faltered at the first hurdle and was bundled out of the play-offs with a 14-7 loss to Canberra. Cliff had played his last game for Manly. Or had he? 'Not only did I know that he would make a comeback but I openly predicted it,' says Colin Lyons enthusiastically. 'I have nothing to do with Manly or the football club but I just knew that he would be back in 1999.'

At the Manly-Warringah RLFC Annual General Meeting in December 1998, rugby league legend Rex Mossop criticised the club for not retaining Cliff Lyons for the coming season. Mossop, who built a career on his blunt but forthright views on the game, stated, 'In my 50 years being involved in rugby league and rugby union, (Cliff) is the smartest, cleverest player I have seen.' Age, he argued, should not be a consideration if Cliff was playing better than the other players and the Sea Eagles should have kept him on their books.

In January 1999, Cliff Lyons turned out in the unfamiliar playing strip of green and white when he guested for Warringah in the Sydney Sevens Tournament at Pittwater Rugby Park. It seems Warringah Rugby Union coach John Briggs shared Rex Mossop's view and grabbed Cliff's services for the knockout competition. Lyons played in the 16-team local club competition run in conjunction with the international tournament in which Commonwealth Gold Medal winner New Zealand defeated Australia. The veteran 37 year-old starred in the Green Rats' 21-10 win over Manly, his cross field running and trademark short passing a highlight of the game.

Warringah was beaten in the semi-final by the Canberra Vikings. Lyons said after the tournament that although his appearance was a 'one-off', he refused to concede that this flirtation with Rugby Union signaled an end to his rugby league career. 'I'll play if they (Manly) want me to,' he was quoted as saying. Lyons was in charge of the club's Under 17's representative team and was never far away from Brookvale Oval in his capacity as Development Officer.

The Sea Eagles opened their season in disastrous fashion; losses to Newcastle (41-6) and Sydney City (46-0) exposing a lack of depth in the club. Injuries to Neil Tierney, Jim Serdaris, Steve Menzies, Damien Driscoll and Anthony Colella seriously eroded Manly's forward strength. As early as March, with Manly winless after three matches and with injuries to backs Luke Phillips and Adam Hayden, there was talk in the press that Lyons would make his return.

The Sea Eagles' assistant coach Peter Sharp, who started his coaching career at Maitland before progressing through Newcastle's junior representative teams (SG Ball, 1988-90, and 'Jersey' Flegg, 1991-93), had won lower grade premierships with Newcastle (1995) and Parramatta (1997) before coming to Manly. 'The plan was to have twelve months as assistant coach to "Boz"' (Fulton), just to find my feet and find out how the club works before taking over as coach in 2000. We were struggling with injuries, particularly the halves and in a few other key areas, and "Boz"' said to me one day that we were going to bring Cliffy back. I thought he was joking,' Sharp admits. 'Cliff had done a little bit of fitness work but not too much; a bit of touch football here and there, but very little preparation for playing. I thought it was outrageous at the time but "Boz"' brought him in and Cliff did a fitness test and played four days later against Newcastle. It absolutely amazed me.'

'In 1999 we were in desperate straits with injuries,' Bob Fulton says in his characteristic forthright manner, 'and so I opted for Cliffy because I knew that he wouldn't let anyone down.'

Lyons made his return to training in the week leading up to the Round 4 clash against Newcastle at Marathon Stadium. Cliff was tentative at first about joining the boys after a month on the sidelines, but when Nik Kosef grabbed him in a friendly bear-hug on the first night of training, he knew that he was back where he belonged. Cliff was also forced to admit to himself that he missed the game a lot more than he thought he would - and a lot more than he was willing to show.

While Cliff's return to Manly was widely anticipated, it still came as a surprise to wife Karen. 'Cliff told me the night before,' Karen says with a wry smile. 'It was a shock because in my mind, we were all retired – the kids and I as well. I thought Cliff was too - but there was still the need for him to play.'

Lyons' return created a media storm of interest. Peter Peters, the club's Media Officer, wrote at the time, 'It's incredible to think that 37-year-old veteran can be the major talking point in a sport that attracts massive electronic and print media. Radio stations from as far north as Cairns and as far west as Perth have sought and been given interviews. Newspaper journalists from New Zealand have been among the 36 requests for one-on-one interviews on the inside story on his incredible comeback. The old bloke has charisma....no doubt about it.'

Manly was very close to its salary cap limit so the cupboard was bare when it came to ironing out a contract. While it would have been fair to say that Cliff probably would have played for nothing, Manly ended up re-signing the veteran five-eighth for far less than $3,000 per match that was reported in the press. As far as Cliff was concerned, money was not an issue. 'I just wanted to play and contribute something to the club,' he says. 'Manly was doing it tough with injuries and I still felt I had something to offer. "Bozo" asked me to play and I wanted to get back on to the field.'

However, when the media produced headlines such as 'Cut-Price

Cliffy' and 'Petty Cash Maestro' it rankled Karen Lyons. 'The media made such a big issue about it that it almost became embarrassing,' she admits. 'It wasn't what he set out to do. It was so demeaning because he was trying to help out his club. In the end, Cliff was able to pass some career milestones so his return benefited both parties.'

Peter Sharp had not seen a transformation like it. 'Cliff's not a magnificent athlete but he's a magnificent football player and he's in a lot better shape than most people think. He looks after himself and although his fitness is not outstanding, he's smart enough, clever enough and cunning enough to get around a football field. From the moment he came back there was a decided improvement in the performance of the team. Against a quality side like Newcastle, Cliff immediately played an up-tempo game and almost turned it around for us.'

The Knights led 16-0 at half-time before Lyons found his old timing and turned the game into a real contest. After intercepting a pass after a Knight's scrum win and saving a certain try, he set up a try for fullback Andrew King and put up the 'bomb' that led to Terry Hill scoring. The scores may have been equalled soon after but King could not hold on to Lyons' pass and a try went begging. Although Newcastle skipped away to eventually win 32-16, Cliff was back with a vengeance.

'It's great to be back,' Cliff said after his return match. 'I hurt all over but it's a good feeling, if you know what I mean.'

The problem remained though; Manly was still not winning. Losses to Souths and Canberra finally brought matters to a head. Although selected to play against Balmain in the next match, halfback Craig Field successfully sought a release from the club. Field, who had never found favour with the club, signed a three-year contract with the Tigers and incredibly turned out for his new club in the Round 7 match against the Sea Eagles. Field produced a man-of-the-match performance to inspire Balmain to an 18-12 win. The situation was then compounded by a lack of discipline off the field, with four players fined $5,000 for an incident in the infamous Sydney nightclub, the Bourbon and Beefsteak Bar. If Cliff, who was one of the four players fined, needed a reminder that the media was willing to latch onto any indiscretion off the field, this was it.

After seven straight losses, Bob Fulton – the man who surpassed a record 400 club games in his coaching career (1979-82 with Easts, 1983-88 and 1993-99 with Manly), announced that he was standing down because of professional and personal reasons. 'The team wasn't winning and there was enormous pressure on "Boz"' externally,' recalls Peter Sharp who stepped into the top job at Manly. 'Bob made his decision for the betterment of the club. He certainly didn't deserve to go out with seven straight losses.'

At the end of a contentious week, the Manly club responded to the pressure in the best way that it knew – by winning on the football field. Manly defeated Parramatta 12-6 with Peter Sharp humbly declaring after the match, 'There was a lot of "Bozo" in that win tonight'. Manly scored first through a try to Nick Kosef but it was the deftly timed pass from Lyons which found Steve Menzies running through the gap that brought back memories of previous years. Manly led 12-0 and then held off a concerted Parramatta fightback with a newfound resolve in defense.

Sharp was able put his own stamp on the club with the Sea Eagles defeating Penrith and North Queensland in the next two matches. In regard to Cliff's return, Sharp said, 'He's very well respected. The players lifted as soon as he came back into the side. It's charisma, ability and attitude. It's everything – he just has an *air* about him. A lot of the more established players - "Beaver" Menzies, Daniel Gartner, Geoff Toovey and Nik Kosef grew up with Cliffy in the side and they certainly had a spring in their step when he returned. All those things added up to assist the changeover of coaches.'

Drama though, was never far away at Manly in 1999. Following the win over Parramatta, John Hopoate was sent home from training after he turned up suffering the effects of a hangover. Sensing that this could mean the end of Hopoate's career rather than the solution to his problem, the Manly players signed a petition organised by Terry Hill appealing to the club not to terminate his contract. Hopoate was fined $10,000, dropped to First Division for eight weeks and ordered to seek counselling.

'That support (of Hopoate by his team-mates) is typical of any football side and I'd be disappointed if it *didn't* happen,' Sharp says. 'What impressed me more was that John hasn't had a drink since, and at the end of the day, like it or not, it has probably turned his life around in some way, shape or form. So that's a positive for the Manly club and for John Hopoate because he was on a downhill spiral heading out of the game.'

With Manly battling to regain form during a mid-season slump in which it won one match out of six, news of a potential merger with the Bears resurfaced, adding further distraction. On May 4, Manly announced that it would entertain the idea of a joint venture with Norths if the Bears were excluded from the Year 2000 competition. By July 1, Ken Arthurson publicly expressed his reservations about Manly's future as a stand-alone club.

'Manly was originally very reluctant to merge and personally I never ever felt that any of the clubs should have *had* to merge,' says Arthurson. 'But the fact of the matter is, due to circumstances over the past five years, and that News Ltd have been supporting clubs financially, this simply broke the back of the ARL clubs. Norths, Souths, Wests, Balmain and Manly have all but gone broke trying to 'go the pace' financially. Manly saw the writing on the wall with a deficit of $2.6 million and probably could have struggled on for another couple of years because they were able to sell property that they owned back to the Leagues Club but what happens after that?'

'When the 14 teams were finally chosen, and Norths and Souths got the chop, Manly extended a lifeline to Norths because, despite all this talk about enmity between the two clubs, it was a long-term decision rather than a short term solution. By offering a lifeline to Norths, we secured our future. It wasn't until the final weeks of the competition that the club decided to do it.'

It was a situation Peter Sharp never even entertained when he accepted the job at Manly. 'At the beginning of the year, a merger with Norths wasn't even on the cards. After a difficult first year trying to remain focused on the club's on-field performances, you have the merger situation where it became apparent that some of the players were not going to be at the club next year. But I absolutely understood the logic of it. It was an absolute necessity. Manly and Norths still have their own identity in First Division and it secures not only the clubs' long-term futures but also the careers of a lot of people.'

Late in the season, Manly regained winning form with a last-minute victory over North Queensland. Cliff Lyons started the match following a further injury to Adam Hayden and set up two late tries to give the Sea Eagles a 28-26 win. For the next match, against Western Suburbs at Brookvale Oval, Cliff retained his place in Manly's starting line-up in what was touted as his 300th first grade appearance for the club. (Lyons had actually passed that mark in the 32-4 loss to Cronulla at Shark Park but the Wests match at Brookvale was a better opportunity to promote the record). Lyons became only the second player in history to play 300 games for the one club following his friend and former Leeds team-mate Andrew Ettingshausen, who achieved the feat the previous month at Cronulla.

An appreciative crowd of 11,890 saw a vintage Cliff Lyons put on five of the nine Manly tries scored as the Sea Eagles humbled Wests, 48-32. It was also fitting that Steve Menzies, a player with whom Cliff formed a great affinity, crossed for his 100th career try in the same match. Despite intermittent rain, the loyal Brookvale Oval fans stayed to the end, with Lyons receiving the game ball from NRL Chief Neil Whittaker before enjoying another lap of honour at the conclusion of the match.

'It really struck home to us how loved Cliff was at Brookvale when the entire crowd remained to watch him complete his lap,' says Cliff's father-in-law Kevin Luff who again made the familiar trip from Gundagai to Brookvale this one last time. 'They lined the fence to shake his hand and to a man, stood to applaud him.' Kevin and Connie Luff took a momento from Brookvale Oval that afternoon – a huge sign left behind by one of Cliff's many fans. 'One one side it said "Congratulations Cliff on your 300th Game" but when you turned it around, on the back was written, "Father Time doesn't know where Cliffy lives!"'

'I doubt if we will ever see another Cliffy in our lifetime,' wrote former team-mate Des Hasler in his column in the *Northern Beaches Weekender* shortly before Cliff's retirement. 'He is a rare individual when it comes to raw talent. He has so much time on the field to weave his magic. The game has become too structured to allow a player the license to run the show like Cliff does at Manly.'

Manly continued its late season surge in form, defeating potential merger partners Norths 28-22. Lyons crossed for one of Manly's four tries in the win at North Sydney, a match in which it seemed increasingly more likely to be the last played between the two clubs. On July 15, Norths and Manly formally reconsidered their respective positions on a joint-merger in light of the decision of Western Suburbs and Balmain to merge for the year 2000. As the club enjoyed a bye before it took on Penrith, it was rocked by further allegations of poor off-field behaviour by its players. Test forward Nik Kosef was subsequently cleared of any wrong-doing in a Gold Coast nightclub incident in which a patron suffered a broken arm but Manly was thrashed 52-10 at Penrith Park.

'It was clear that we needed to make some changes and that some of the players had been at the club too long,' Sharp says. While some decisions were easy; 'Terry Hill's move to the Western Tigers was purely a financial decision – they offered him more money and we couldn't match it,' Sharp says. 'But the decision to let Cliff go was the hardest decision I've had to make at the club. Towards the end of the season I had a quiet chat to him after training one night and said that it was time to retire. His legs were still pumping but now the opposition was catching up with him. The interchange rule had lengthened his career but now judicious replacements were not enough.'

In July, leading Foxtel statistician Ian Collis produced the incredible finding that in five run on games and nine matches off the bench, Lyons had set up 17 tries for his team – second only in total to Newcastle's Andrew Johns who had played in 15 complete games. Coach Peter Sharp may have felt a commitment to blood his younger players and use Cliff in a supporting role, but this statistic confirms what everyone already knew about Cliff - that he was a match-winner, a champion.

Manly defeated Balmain 44-14 after the Tigers led 12-0, before playing its final match at Brookvale. Against Brisbane, Cliff proved his class one last time for the fans. The Sea Eagles fought back from a 26-4 deficit to clinch a 26-all draw against the Broncos with Cliff fittingly scoring a try in his final appearance at the oval. In honour of his last match at the ground, the Lyons brothers erected a make-shift sign near their favourite spot under the scoreboard, 'The Cliff Lyons Family Hill' - an obviously pointed reminder to the Manly Club after the decision by Cronulla to rename its grandstand in honour of Andrew Ettingshausen. 'The Brookvale crowds were great and the support they showed Cliff was fantastic,' says Karen Lyons. 'In his last match at the ground, there were people from Bathurst and Newcastle who said that they had come just to see Cliff play his final match. It was just amazing.'

Cliff's final first grade match – his 309th for Manly and the 332nd in his 15-season career, was against St George-Illawarra at Wollongong's WIN Stadium on August 28, 1999. In a match which also marked the departure of Cliff's 1990 Kangaroo team-mate Brad Mackay, St George led 20-8 before a belated Manly fightback saw the Sea Eagles fail by just two points. A week later, Cliff was informed that he would be among five first graders, (along with Tierney, Serdaris, Hopoate and Phil Adamson) who would not be offered contracts if a merger went ahead. On September 8, Manly and Norths made a formal approach to the NRL to enter into a joint venture and by Ocotber 1, the deal was complete. Cliff Lyons' NRL career was effectively over.

At year's end, Cliff was afforded the honour of captaining an Australian Aboriginal team in an unofficial 'Test' against Papua-New Guinea. Coached by legendary Australian Test forward Arthur Beetson and managed by St George great Ricky Walford, the Australian Aborigines thrashed the Kumuls 58-12 in the First 'Test' at Campbelltown before Cliff deputised for injured captain John Simon in the return match at Barlow Park, Cairns. While in camp for the two-match series, Cliff travelled to Wrest Point Casino in Hobart to receive a National Aboriginal and Torres Strait Islander Sports Award. While Cathy Freeman was named National Sportswoman of the Year for the fourth consecutive time, Cliff tied with AFL Champion Nicky Winmar as National Sportsman of the Year.

In accepting the 7th Annual Award, Cliff modestly thanked his family for their support during his long career. 'It all comes back to my family who have stuck by me all the way through my rugby league career. My family has been supportive of everything I've done.' Looking toward the future he said, 'At this stage, now it's up to us athletes in the higher standard to bring the kids through. It's the right time to get involved with the children and help them out as much as we can.'

A week after celebrating his 38th birthday, and captaining a team that included experienced first graders Own Craigie (Newcastle), Albert Torrens (Manly), Kevin McGuinness (Wests), John Buttigieg (North Queensland) and Dennis Moran (Parramatta), Cliff played the final representative match of his career. In front of an appreciative home crowd of 5200, Cliff led his team to an authoritative 32-10 victory. The opportunity to captain the Australian Aborigines also gave him the chance to finally mend some bridges with Arthur Beetson, who all those years ago had twice missed out on having Cliff play in his team.

Although it came in the eleventh hour of his career, Cliff also achieved his career goal of playing in a 'Test' match on home-soil in front of his family. For the Campbelltown match, the Luff family travelled up from Gundagai to cheer him on. In Cairns conducting a seminar in her work as an Aboriginal Health Officer, Cliff's mother Melva was also in the crowd that night to see her son play what was thought to be the final match of his career.

But, as with most things, Cliff had different ideas on the issue.

CHAPTER FIFTEEN

The Future

As the playing career of one generation of the Lyons family appeared to be ending, another generation, that of Cliff's son Shane, was just moving into top gear. After receiving an Indigenous Althletics Scholarship in November 1996 and playing for the Canberra Cosmos in 1997-98, Shane left Australia with Lachlan Wright of Sydney Olympic in August 1998 to trial with leading Portuguese soccer club Benfica. The pair spent a month in Lisbon training under the guidance of former Scottish international Graeme Souness, but a combination of the language barrier and homesickness saw Shane move to England. At Coventry, work permit problems dashed his hopes of playing professional soccer in England. 'I ended up playing for an amateur side there but there was still the existing problem of trying to obtain a work permit,' Shane told the *Telegraph's* John Taylor. 'I decided to come back home and rang the Spirit and asked them if I could trial.'

Shane now lives with Cliff and Karen while playing soccer in Sydney. So, is watching his son play soccer at North Sydney Oval, where Cliff had strutted his stuff fifteen years earlier a case of *Back to the Future*? 'Yeah, a little bit,' Cliff says with a broad grin. 'It's a like old times at

North Sydney when we go and watch Shane play, except of course, he's playing soccer,' he adds, shaking his head. 'Matty's also plays soccer in the Manly area. I've had a chat to him about switching to League but he wants to keep playing with his mates so, fair enough.'

In 1999 Cliff's mother Melva Kennedy, a self-educated single mother of six children who left school at age 14 to support her family, graduated with an Advanced Diploma in Health from Batchelor College in the Northern Territory which specialises in training and tertiary education for Aboriginal and Torres Strait Islander peoples. For several years now, Melva has worked in child sexual assault counselling and community education and training with indigenous people. The first aboriginal person accredited to conduct the Protective Behaviours Program she has held training workshops on dealing with child sexual assault throughout New South Wales, the Northern Territory and in Canberra. At the end of that year, Melva was awarded a Churchill Fellowship to go to Canada and study indigenous approaches to dealing with child abuse, sexual assault and domestic violence.

By any measurement, Cliff's mother is an incredible person whose professional career has had a significant impact on the lives of her children. 'Mum's achievements certainly influenced the rest of us into going into Aboriginal Health Care,' says Colin Lyons, 'and I also think that a lot of it also comes from Cliff's success as well. He's been out there for years doing what he does best – showing the way for Aboriginal people, and we're out there doing our bit, giving something back to the Aboriginal community. The seed was planted by Cliff's success in rugby league.'

When Melva Kennedy worked for the Aboriginal Medical Service in the early 1990s, Cliff's sister Narelle and older brother Rick also joined the service and completed an Aboriginal Health Worker's course. Rick works in the NSW Ambulance Service as an Aboriginal employment officer, Narelle is employed by the Aboriginal Housing

Commission, Nita works in the childcare industry and Darren works with the Aboriginal Health Service in Bega. Colin, who used to be a Drug and Alcohol counsellor, currently works with Aboriginal kids at Bonnyrigg.

'The success Cliff has achieved has done a lot for our family and for me in particular,' Colin admits. 'For a long time I had a chip on my shoulder about Cliff's success not opening doors for the rest of us. I played a trial for Manly when I was 22 after Cliff had signed with the club in 1986. Although I played well, I got knocked out cold on my feet and missed out on being graded. I was running around on instinct and didn't know where I was. I couldn't remember anything about the game but my brother Rick told me I had played well and deserved to be picked. I was dirty at first but it turned out to be the turning point of my life.'

'I was a young bloke with alcohol problems who was getting into trouble with the law but once Cliff made it into first grade, I realised I had to wake up to myself for the sake of Cliff and the rest of the family. I had a responsibility not to let anyone down. Although I knew I had the talent and deserved to be given a chance in grade, it was lucky that I didn't get selected. I booked myself into 'rehab' and stayed there for nine months and by the time I got out, Cliff was setting the world on fire at Manly. During the hard times, Cliff's success held me up and encouraged me to get through 'rehab' and to make the most of my life.'

In February 2000, Cliff's father Patrick Lyons passed away after a long illness. In a moving service at Narrandera, on the banks of the Murrumbidgee River, Pat Lyons was laid to rest in a simple, open-air service in which each of the Lyons children took turns to remember their father. Colin Lyons, a car enthusiast who with his father's help meticulously remodelled his prized utility, paid Pat the compliment of driving his coffin to the service in the back of the ute – the hearse trailing behind at a respectable distance.

In many ways, life has turned full circle for Cliff Lyons. Six months after he said goodbye to Brookvale Oval, the desire to be involved in rugby league has not diminished. 'There is a whole new generation of players coming through who need to learn how I play, "off the cuff",' he says. In 1999, Cliff took on the role of coach of Manly's S.G. Ball side before returning to the field and this year sees him in charge of the club's Under 18s representative team. The Manly club has a great track record of starting its ex-players along the road to coach – Ken Arthurson, Ron Willey, Terry Randall, Max Krilich, Allan Thompson, Bob Fulton; and Cliff is embarking on that journey now.

Peter Sharp, Cliff's last coach at Manly says, 'The challenge now for Cliff is to be able to tap into that deep body of knowledge that he has about the game and to learn how to impart that to others. At the end of the day, it's going to be difficult to explain to younger players how he does what he does on the football field but he has a great relationship with kids in the area and whenever he visits the schools, the kids just love him. He's always got a story for them and they hang on to his every word.'

'Since the merger, as opposed to Manly being out of the competition, kids in the area will have a career path to the Northern Eagles via SG Ball, Jersey Flegg, President's Cup and First Division - and that's the most important issue,' says Sharp. 'Cliff can play a big role in assisting the kids in the local area and hopefully, he'll play a big part in helping the Manly-Warringah club maintain its rugby league profile in the area. He has a very special place in my heart in that in my first year of coaching I got to work closely with him. My only regret is that I didn't get the chance to coach him ten years ago.'

Bob Fulton agrees. 'I see his future with the Manly club rather than the joint venture, teaching kids what he knows about the game. He is strong in all areas of the game and has a lot to offer. The role of the assistant coach is now a very important one in the modern game. A great job for Cliff would be as a skills coach – especially working with the halves. Given his background and what he's achieved, I would like to see the NRL utilise Cliff's standing in the Aboriginal community in a liaison capacity. Cliff's got the whole package – he has the skill, the charisma and the family support to really make a difference.'

'My hope for Cliff is that he is able to teach other kids his ability,' says his mother Melva. 'The NRL should ensure that his skills are not lost and that kids all over the country get the opportunity to learn what he knows. In my mind, Cliff has been underpaid and undervalued during his career. Some people, especially in the country, have traded in on his celebrity status and taken advantage of his easy-going nature. Cliff has never used his celebrity status as a first grade footballer for his own advantage.'

'Cliff could play for another five years – given the chance he would play until his legs couldn't carry him anymore,' says Melva. 'I was disappointed that the merger didn't offer him a contract but you can't blame them – there's not a lot of demand for 38-year-old footballers. Cliff just wants to play.' There was a real chance that Cliff would have played for Souths in 2000 if the Rabbitoh's appeal against its exclusion from the NRL had been successful. Not because he didn't appreciate everything Manly had done for him but because he just wants any opportunity to get out onto the field and play. Although this wasn't meant to be, Cliff fielded offers from Gundagai and the Central Coast before deciding to put on the boots again and play for Umina.

'Cliff understands not being able to play for Manly anymore but I believe that he should still be allowed to play for whoever he wants,' says Karen Lyons. 'Playing for Umina is fun, the way it used to be with Manly. Rather than being criticised for coming out of "retirement", he should be praised for having the guts to get out onto the field.'

Melva especially used to enjoy the weekend ritual of travelling with Karen, Cliff and the kids to suburban Sydney grounds to watch her son play and still makes the trip to Umina, north of Sydney. However, there were drawbacks. 'I used to go to Cliff's matches as much as possible but the abuse from sections of the crowd used to get too much,' she says. 'I used to sit there with my radio headphones on my head, listening to Ray Hadley call the match on 2UE to drown out the noise.' Melva has a special affinity for mothers who have to watch their sons play rugby league. She adds, 'I can only imagine what Mrs Toovey has had to go through with the injuries Geoff has had to endure during his career.'

It is a fact of life that things change. The Manly club has always intimated that there will be a place for Cliff after his playing career ended but the economic reality following the club's merger means that this situation is tenuous at best. Cliff will remain with Manly for half the week, fulfilling his duties as Development Officer and junior representative coach, but his services have also been secured by David Liddiard, CEO of the National Aboriginal Sports Corporation Association. NASCA, which relies heavily on corporate sector sponsorship from groups such as Lend Lease, Westpac, Aussie Home Loans, Harvey Norman and the ARL, predominantly caters to netball and rugby league but has recently added a golf professional to their team and will soon be looking at basketball. NASCA also works with the Australian National Training Authority to arrange Sports Traineeships and has assisted in placing more than ninety Sports Trainees.

The departure of former Souths captain Darrell Trindall to play in England at the end of 1999 led to Cliff's recruitment by NASCA to take charge of its 'We'll Find You' Rugby League program. David Liddiard explains the reasons behind the move. 'I was a bit skeptical at first because Cliff is such a quiet guy but he came highly recommended by the Manly club. Marty Gurr and Frank Stanton spoke of the great job he has done as a Development Officer in the

Manly area. We came to an agreement to share Cliff's services - Manly two days and NASCA three days.'

'We go out to the small towns and identify talent,' says Liddiard. 'These players are added to our database and invited to attend development camps that we conduct four times a year. We recently had a three-day camp at Narrabeen. Usually, the first player asked to come out for a visit is Cliff Lyons. He is by far one of the most popular rugby league players in the bush.' And Liddiard's hopes for Cliff in the future? 'I'd like Cliff to really take control of the "We'll Find You" program and concentrate on what he's going to do with life after league. He has the personality and credibility to reach out to young Aboriginal players in the bush. Cliff's an unassuming guy who's done it all.'

Cliff has always made himself available for Aboriginal representative teams, helping out where he can and when club commitments allowed. 'Cliff played for the Blacktown Koori Eels in 1998-99 but we lost both years to Redfern All Blacks,' says Colin Lyons. 'That sort of thing – a high-profile player like Cliff playing in a Koori competition breaks down all sorts of barriers and opens up doors for kids from the bush. In my mind, Cliff's been underrated not only as a professional footballer but also as an Australian sportsman.'

Colin Lyons and Bob Fulton both draw the comparison between Cliff's career and that of Australia's best known indigenous athlete, Cathy Freeman. 'Cliff doesn't have to go and wave the (Aboriginal) flag for us, Cathy does that really well,' says Colin. 'Cliff just goes out and tries to be himself, and that's what he does best.' Fulton adds, 'The point about Cliff and Cathy Freeman is that they both go about their profession – Cathy albeit at an international level and Cliff here at home, quietly and humbly. In their own way, they're both great role models for young Australians.'

In January, Cliff was asked to be the Year 2000 Australia Day Ambassador for Gundagai. Local Mayor Len Tozer, Cliff's former rugby league mentor with the Gundagai Tigers, presided over the civic ceremony at Carberry Park, with Cliff presenting Australia Day plaques to the town's Citizen of the Year and Young Citizen of the Year as well as the Sports Achiever Award. Cliff's speech was suitably simple yet moving.

'I love coming back to Gundagai,' Cliff was quoted as saying, 'and this town and its people will always have a special place in my heart. It was in Gundagai that I met my wife Karen, and it was Gundagai which gave me a real start to my career in rugby league. Australia Day is about national identity, but for me Australia Day in Gundagai is special. Gundagai has the great Australian quality for friendship in greater measure than anywhere I know. Australia Day is a celebration of those things which are good in our nation. And the best Australian thing of the lot is the type of friendship we find in Gundagai.'

'I am grateful that I was able to play for Australia. But in our own way we all play for Australia, we all have our own roles to play in making this a truly great nation. And all over Australia, there are people doing their bit to make our country a better place.'

Recently, Cliff has been asked to lend his name to a cause that affects all Australians. In the Year 2000, he will be an Ambassador for Aboriginal Literacy and Numeracy. For a kid who was actually encouraged to leave school to further his sporting career, Cliff has learnt the value of staying in school and getting a good education.

It is not the least bit important to Cliff Lyons how he will be remembered. 'Cliff was unfortunate in that his career peaked in an era of great five-eighths – Lewis, Kenny and Lamb,' says Ken Arthurson. 'He had to bide his time and was a late maturer to international rugby league. But let me say this – he was certainly up there with the best of them. He was simply top class.' Arthurson adds, 'When Cliff received Life Membership at the Annual General Meeting of the Manly-Warringah Football Club in December 1999,

I congratulated him and said that if ever I was in a position to pick a best ever Manly team, Cliff Lyons would have to be in the side.'

With the merger of Manly-Warringah and the North Sydney club, the irony is that more than any other player in the 1990s, Cliff Lyons is the one who became synonymous with what Ken Arthurson described as "Manly *style* and Manly *success*". Those Brookvale Oval veterans who will sit with their grandchildren and recall the dashing manner in which the Sea Eagles used to play, will remember the sight of the champion five-eighth scurrying through a gap, holding his pass to the final moment, and then sending a team-mate in for the try. Invariably, Cliff would be the first player on hand to congratulate his team-mates, flashing that big smile of his and waving to the crowd.

Rival coaches, people as diverse in their approach to the game as Warren Ryan, Roy Masters or Phil Gould, have publicly lauded Cliff's ability as a player. In an interview I conducted with Ryan in the early 1990s, the premiership-winning coach hammered home the following point; 'The thing about rugby league is that guys from more affluent environments find it harder to be successful than the blokes from tougher backgrounds. There are anomalies and contradictions to rules, but for guys from under-privileged backgrounds, the game is made for them.....not tennis or golf. Give me the back street Newtown kid or the bloke from the country who wants to make it in the city because they don't want to go home a failure.'

In the unique playing career of Clifford Patrick Lyons, rugby league found the best of both worlds – the kid from the back streets *and* the boy from the bush. The only difference to Warren Ryan's assertion is that in Cliff's particular case, he was never concerned about failure.

The word failure has never been part of Cliff's make-up.

Records and Statistics

Cliff Lyons: Factfile

Name: *Clifford Patrick Lyons*
Born: *October 19, 1961*
Place: *Narrandera, NSW*

Playing Career

1981:   *Cronulla-Sutherland (Under 23's)*
1982-84:   *Gundagai Tigers (Group 9)*
1985:   *North Sydney*
            Leeds (England) 1985-86
1986-99:   *Manly-Warringhah*
            Sheffield Eagles (England) 1986-87
            Leeds (England) 1988-89

Representative Honours

1982:   *Combined Riverina - Caltex Country Champions*
1983:   *Combined Riverina*
1984:   *Combined Riverina*

1985:   *City Seconds*
1987:   *NSW State of Origin (Third & Fourth matches)*
1988:   *City Origin*
            NSW State of Origin (First & Third matches)
1989:   *'Rest of the World' v. Great Britain*
1990:   *City Origin*
            AUSTRALIA – 1990 Kangaroo Tour of England and France
1991:   *NSW State of Origin (First & Second matches)*
            AUSTRALIA – 1991 Kangaroo Tour of Papua-New Guinea
1992:   *City Seconds and City Origin (replacement)*
1996:   *Aboriginal Dream Team (Coca-Cola World Sevens)*
1999:   *Australian Aborigines versus Papua-New Guinea*

Awards

1987:   *Clive Churchill Medal – 'Player of the Grand Final'*
            2GB 'Player of the Year'
            Sun 'Player of the Year'
            Manly-Warringah 'Player of the Year'
1990:   *Gold Dally M 'Player of the Year'*
            Gold Dally M 'Five-Eighth of the Year'
            Manly-Warringah 'P&O Player of the Year'
1994:   *Gold Dally M 'Player of the Year'*
            Gold Dally M 'Five-Eighth of the Year'
            2UE 'Player of the Year'
            Rugby League Week 'Player of the Year'
1995:   *Runner-Up Gold Dally M 'Player of the Year'*
            Doug Daley Memorial Trophy as Clubman of the Year
1999:   *National Aboriginal and Torres Strait Islander Sport Awards - Aboriginal Sportsman of the Year (tied with Nicky Winmar)*

Career Statistics

Club/Year	Games/ (repl)	Tries	Goals	Field Goals	Points
North Sydney*(1985):*	**23 (0 repl)**	7	4	1	37
Manly *(1986 - 1999):*	**254(55 repl)**	80	5	6	336
1986:	20 (0 repl)	5		1	21
1987:	21 (1 repl)	7		1	29
1988:	22 (0 repl)	14			56
1989:	20 (1 repl)	9			36
1990:	24 (0 repl)	7	3		34
1991:	17 (2 repl)	2	2	1	13
1992:	22 (0 repl)	4			12
1993:	10 (8 repl)	2			8
1994:	23 (0 repl)	7		3	31
1995:	25 (0 repl)	9			36
1996:	20 (5 repl)	4			16
1997:	8 (15 repl)	7			28
1998:	12 (13 repl)	1			4
1999:	10 (10 repl)	2			8

Club Totals (15 seasons) - 277 (55 repl) = 332 games (87 tries, 9 goals, 7fg - 373pts)

Representative Matches

Rep Team/Yr		Games/Repl	Tries	Goals	Field Goals	Points
City II	*1985:*	1			1	1
City Origin	*1988:*	1				
City Origin	*1991:*	1				
City Firsts	*1992:*	1				
City Origin	*1992:*	1 (repl)				

City (1985, 1988 & 1991-92) 4 games (1 repl) – 1fg (1pt)

Rep Team/Yr		Games/Repl	Tries	Goals	Field Goals	Points
NSW	*1987:*	2		1		4
NSW	*1988:*	2				
NSW	*1991:*	2				

NSW (1987-88 & 1991) 6 games – 1t (4pts)

Rep Team/Yr	Games/Repl	Tries	Goals	Field Goals	Points
Australia 1990:	**4 Tests**	1			**4**
v. Great Britian	2 Tests	1			4
v. France	4 Tests				
Tour games in					
England/France	4 games	3			12
Australia 1991:	**2 Tests**	1			**4**
v. Papua-New Guinea	2 Tests	1			4
Tour games in					
Papua-New Guinea	3 games	2			8

Australia (1990-91) 6 Tests – 2t (8pts), 7 tour games – 5t (20pts).

Bibliography:

Harris, Bret   *Winfield State of Origin: 1980-1991* – Sun
                      Australia (Pan Macmillan), Sydney (1992).

Heads, Ian   *True Blue: The Story of the NSWRL* - Iron
                      Bark Press, Paddington (1992).

Madigan, John   *The Maher Cup and Tumut* – Wilkie Watson
                      Publications, Tumut (1995).

Madigan, John   *Tumut's Roddy Shield* – Wilkie Watson
                      Publications, Tumut (1997).

Masters, Roy   *Inside League* – Pan, Sydney (1990)

McGregor, Adrian   *Simply the Best* – UQP, Brisbane (1990)

Middleton, David   *Rugby League 1987-88, 1988-89, 1989-90 &*
                      1990-91 – Lester-Townsend, Paddington.

Middleton, David   *Rugby League 1991-92* - Playright
                      Publishing, Carringbah (1992).

Middleton, David   *Rugby League 1992-93* and *1994* - Iron Bark Press, Paddington.

Middleton, David   *Rugby League 1995, 1996, 1997, 1998, 1999 & 2000* Harper Collins, Sydney.

Whiticker, Alan   *Grand Finals of the NSWRL* – Gary Allen, Smithfied (1992, 1994 & 1997).

Whiticker, Alan   *The Terry Lamb Story* - Gary Allen, Smithfield (1992).

Whiticker, Alan &   *The Story of the North Sydney 'Bears'* -
Anderson, Greg   Sherborne - Sutherland Publishing, Loftus (1988).

Whiticker, Alan &   *Rugby League Test Matches in Australia* -
Collis, Ian   ABC Enterprises, Sydney (1994)

Whiticker, Alan   *The Encyclopedia of Rugby League Players*
Hudson, Glen   Gary Allen, Smithfield (1993, 1995 & 1999)